SpringerBriefs in Economics

SpringerBriefs present concise summaries of cutting-edge research and practical applications across a wide spectrum of fields. Featuring compact volumes of 50 to 125 pages, the series covers a range of content from professional to academic. Typical topics might include:

- A timely report of state-of-the art analytical techniques
- A bridge between new research results, as published in journal articles, and a contextual literature review
- A snapshot of a hot or emerging topic
- An in-depth case study or clinical example
- A presentation of core concepts that students must understand in order to make independent contributions

SpringerBriefs in Economics showcase emerging theory, empirical research, and practical application in microeconomics, macroeconomics, economic policy, public finance, econometrics, regional science, and related fields, from a global author community.

Briefs are characterized by fast, global electronic dissemination, standard publishing contracts, standardized manuscript preparation and formatting guidelines, and expedited production schedules.

More information about this series at http://www.springer.com/series/8876

Adina Dabu · Paul D. Aligica

Economic Dualism and Agrarian Policies

Land Reforms and Structural Economic Change in Romania, 1864–2000

Springer

Adina Dabu
University of Maryland
College Park, MD, USA

Paul D. Aligica
University of Bucharest
Bucharest, Romania

George Mason University
Fairfax, VA, USA

ISSN 2191-5504 ISSN 2191-5512 (electronic)
SpringerBriefs in Economics
ISBN 978-3-030-47835-3 ISBN 978-3-030-47836-0 (eBook)
https://doi.org/10.1007/978-3-030-47836-0

This Springer imprint is published by the registered company Springer Nature Switzerland AG
The registered company address is: Gewerbestrasse 11, 6330 Cham, Switzerland

Acknowledgements

This book project has been long in the making, and it has been made possible by the support of several academic institutions with which we were associated during this period. We would like to acknowledge and thank in particular to the Virginia Polytechnic Institute and State University, where a part of this project was written by Adina Dabu as a MA thesis in Development Sociology; to the Mercatus Center at George Mason University, where Paul D. Aligica's work on dualism and structural reforms was enthusiastically encouraged and supported; and to the Faculty of Business and Public Administration of the University of Bucharest that made possible the completion of this volume.

A version of Chap. 2 of the book was published as: P. D. Aligica "Structural Constraints: Implications of Economic Dualism for the Development and International Integration of South Eastern Europe", *Journal of South Europe and the Balkans*, Volume 5, Number 3, 2003. We thank Taylor and Francis for giving us the permission to use it.

The book also incorporates parts of A. Dabu and P. D. Aligica "Land Reform and Agricultural Reform Policies in Romania's Transition to the Market Economy: Overview and Assessment", *East European Economics*, Vol. 41, No. 5, 2003. We thank Taylor and Francis for giving us the permission to use it.

Needless to say, while acknowledging and thanking to all those who made this project possible, the authors are solely responsible for the book's content, arguments and conclusions.

Contents

List of Tables

Chapter 1
Introduction

Abstract Taking as a starting point a conceptual framework defined by the topics of dualism, agrarian reforms, structural change policies and their associated ideas and designs, this project is articulating an exploratory contribution to two major themes. First, to the investigation of structural economic change in societies and economies defined by dualism. Second, to the study of policy ideas and policy learning in the context of large-scale policy reform experiments.

Keywords Development theory · Structural change · Economic dualism · Public policy · Agrarian reforms

Over the last century and a half, a constant problem for policymakers in countries of Eastern Europe, including Romania, was how to shrink the agricultural sector while at the same time effectively developing the industry and service sectors to a level comparable to that of more advanced Western nations. The central fact acknowledged by all reformers was that the economic structure and the functioning of their states and political systems were strongly conditioned, if not marred, by a long-lasting feature: their dualism. A dual economy is an economy that has an advanced and a backward sector which, while operating at the same time, remain nevertheless largely disconnected. Such a system comprises two very different sub-systems, where a modern economy co-exists with a traditional, oversized peasant economy and the two, while having contact with each other, are not and cannot be fully integrated.

This structural feature has its origins in late modernization processes and has distinctively shaped the dynamics of the polities and economies in the region. The East European countries do unquestionably share this feature. The difference between the various countries and regions of the world comes in this respect from the degree to which their dualism was overcome or not, and from the measure in which it continues to play a role, either directly or through its legacies. In the case of South Eastern Europe nations, the dualism of their economies remains to this day a key explanatory factor in any attempt to understand the dynamics of the region. Moreover, dualism has always played a crucial role in the process of international integration of South Eastern Europe in the European and global system and it is likely that it will continue to play a role in the future. Thus, it should not come as a surprise that in many respects,

A. Dabu and P. D. Aligica, *Economic Dualism and Agrarian Policies*,
SpringerBriefs in Economics, https://doi.org/10.1007/978-3-030-47836-0_1

overcoming dualism was considered the key to the structural change effort of setting those economies on the path to development and modernization.

As one may expect, agricultural reform policies are crucial in this context. Agriculture is the core of the traditional sector. The problem of agriculture, its role and weight in the structure of the economy, as well as the problem of its links to the other branches and sectors of the economy, has been rightly considered the key challenge of the development process and its associated policies. The ideas shaping the various approaches and strategies engaging this historical task of structurally transforming a social and economic system by reforming and redefining its agricultural sector, has been of momentous importance. Their analysis is hence of crucial relevance, as any serious investigation of this topic must focus on the specific ideas behind the reform strategies and policies.

In doing that, one must move beyond a simplistic "ideas versus material factors" model of social change and policy implementation. If the goal is to better understand the process of social and economic change by sharpening our insight on agricultural policy reform based on a clear understanding of policy ideas (or policy designs) as critical factors in themselves, then the task ahead implies a serious methodological challenge. Addressing these complex relationships between ideas and material, structural and institutional factors, requires a combination of detailed historical and sociological research ("process-tracing"), conceptual clarity, a good grasp of theoretical models and frameworks and a substantial familiarity with their intellectual history. This book is a contribution to this task.

Taking as a starting point a conceptual framework defined by the topics of dualism, agrarian reforms, structural change policies and their associated ideas and designs, this book is articulating an exploratory contribution to two major themes. First, to the investigation of structural economic change in societies and economies defined by dualism. Second, to the study of policy ideas and policy learning in the context of large-scale policy reform experiments. To achieve this goal, the book will focus on one country (Romania), will outline one specific area of interest (agrarian economic policies) and will explore a conceptual area defined by questions such as: What could one learn from the experience in reforming and modernizing the dualist system of Romania? What could one learn from a long-term national level attempt to deal with the problem of dualism and agricultural reform? Have the post-communist policy designers learned something from the pre-1945 policy experiments? Are the post-communist transition and reforms reflecting a learning process as regarding agrarian policy ideas and the modernization of dualist systems? Was there a lesson been learned from the communist experiment as regarding policy design and the concepts and ideas operating in the field of agrarian reform and policies? Was that lesson incorporated in the post-1989 policies?

Let us note at this point that the more general lessons regarding dualism may well be relevant not only for agrarian-industrial dualist situations. Dualism may be seen as a larger phenomenon, in which the dual polarity may be defined in different ways, like, for instance, the industrial-postindustrial one. As such, the insights brought forth by the book may have a larger applicability. Be they insights regarding the evolution and challenge of modernization or insights regarding the nature of policy learning and the function of policy ideas, these insights, illuminate a series of phenomena which are crucial not only in policy studies but also in economic history or development sociology. Hence the inter-disciplinary nature of the book.

As already noted, this book uses the Romanian case as a vehicle. As in the case of other developing countries, Romania tried to solve its development problem by implementing a range of policies based on and inspired by various sociological and economic views, theories and models. It did that on the background defined by the notion of dualism, as a major structural constraint on any modernization policy or strategy initiative. Those policies were only partially successful and at the beginning of the twenty-first century, the problem of underdevelopment and unsatisfactory economic performance of the agrarian sector was still largely unresolved.

This book takes as a starting point the mixed record of the post-communist agricultural reforms prior to the moment Romania was turning all its focus and energies on the objective of accession to the UE, around 2000, and explores the extent to which the reforms taking place over the post-1989 decade were informed by the lessons provided by the set of policies and ideas regarding rural development in both the pre-communist and communist periods. The turn of the century is taken as a key timeline parameter for two reasons. First because around that time the logic of the European accession (integration) has become the dominant logic of the Romanian national policymaking. It was a moment when the exogenous factor overcame the endogenous policy dynamics. Second, that year offers not only a benchmark for closing a historical cycle and opening another one, but it also offers a very telling symbolic milestone for the historical periodization of the case.

To sum up, the approach advanced by the book leads indeed not only to an economic history and development sociology analysis but also to an exercise in policy analysis, framed by the problem of policy learning: the inquiry of whether and how the ideas, concepts, and theories that led to mixed results or downright policy failure in the past are rejected (or correspondingly adjusted) to the new context. In brief, the result is a unique monograph that combines economic history, institutional analysis, with policy analysis by using the specific case study of Romania to explore more general themes of policy design and implementation.

Chapter 2
Framing the Approach

Abstract This chapter articulates the conceptual apparatus to be used in framing and discussing the case of Romanian agrarian reforms. It shows why, in order to understand and evaluate the reform strategies in case, one needs to understand the set of ideas behind them as frameworks inspiring, defining, and designing the specific policies and reform strategies. The chapter demonstrates how that conceptual apparatus connects and integrates via the notion of "learning" the analysis of both the ideas behind policies and the results of those policies, thus, setting the stage for the rest of the book.

Keywords Public policies · Policy theory · Policy learning · Knowledge processes · Governance · Applied social theory

At the core of this book is the notion of policy reforms seen as experiments in applied social and economic thinking and taking place in systems that have structural constraints generated by their dualism. Hence, the book's approach is framed by the vision and conceptual apparatus associated to these concepts. In conjunction, they offer an underlying framework for interpreting, analyzing and understanding the relevant phenomena and cases.

This chapter will be focused on the notion of policy reforms and the ideas behind them. One undeniable feature of public policies and economic and business strategies is the fact that they are ideas-driven phenomenon. These specific ideas—and the ways they are implemented—are key to the success or failure of any public policy. They may not be sufficient conditions for success but, by all accounts, they seem to be necessary conditions. This book takes this reality as vital and builds up its structure and approach around it. The notion of ideas-driven strategies and policies and the associated concepts are the drivers framing the structure and approach of the book and therefore they take preeminence. Hence, the first chapter will be mostly dedicated to them. The next chapter will focus on the notion of dualism as the background on which the book's arguments will operate. Together, this chapter and the next one, are articulating the framework of the general approach of the book.

A. Dabu and P. D. Aligica, *Economic Dualism and Agrarian Policies*,
SpringerBriefs in Economics, https://doi.org/10.1007/978-3-030-47836-0_2

Out of the many possible thematic domains of relevance, the book concentrates on a set of ideas ruling the decision-making in a *specific policy-area*, a set of so called "issue-area doctrines" or "policy paradigms". Policy paradigms structure the very way in which policy-makers see the world and their role (Hall, 1989). More precisely, the study grows out of an interest in the agrarian reform policy paradigms in South Eastern Europe and more exactly, in Romania, from mid-nineteenth century to the period immediately prior to Romania's European Union accession. Their working definition, for the purpose of this study, will be this: The overarching set of theoretical and conceptual economic and sociological ideas that *specify how* the agrarian problems are to be perceived, *which* goals might be attained through policy and *what* sorts of techniques can be used to reach those goals. That is to say, these ideas help to order the worldview of the policy-makers, their understanding of the key problems and of the solutions in the specific area of modernization and agriculture's role in the structure of the economy. By ordering and defining the situation, by postulating causal patterns and by providing compelling ethical or moral motivations for action they define policy goals and guide behavior.

The most important thing to note about them is that they are not purely normative or arbitrary. These are ideas that have at their core *causal beliefs*. *Causal beliefs* are beliefs about cause and effect relationships, and they provide guides on how to achieve objectives or strategies for the attainment of goals that are valued because of shared principled beliefs. As already explained, among the large class of causal beliefs, the project has an interest in the causal beliefs regarding the operation of the agrarian economy and the ways that operation should be reformed or improved in function of a set of implicit beliefs regarding economic development in countries with a dual economic structure.

A corollary of this approach, in which ideas shape policies which are applied in practice as quasi-natural experiments, is the notion of learning. Implied is the view that decision-makers and the communities they represent have the capacity to learn from experience, to analyze and evaluate the results of policy experiments and, by implication, of the doctrines or paradigms or causal beliefs inspiring them. In the context of this study, the link between ideas, in the narrow sense of "causal beliefs" (i.e. beliefs about cause-effect relationships in the realm of agricultural development), and rational learning is definitional. On the one hand, learning could be seen as a form of evolutionary collective process, in which knowledge is produced as an emergent collective property. However, one could also see learning in a more standard way as rational learning, defined as mindful relationship with past experiences, and in this sense rational learning generates causal relationships. Or, put otherwise, inherent in the definition of causal beliefs in public policy is the idea that they have to be based sooner or later in a rational learning process. Our study takes the second route.

In this line of thought, policy experiments (reforms) can be regarded as sequences of coordinated actions that are guided by a set of *ideas* or "strategic notions" (Tomich, Kilby, & Johnson, 1995) in order to generate the desired policy *consequences*. The set of expected, and often-unexpected policy consequences can be ultimately regarded as *lessons* that might further inspire and guide new policy experiments. To be more concrete, the book starts by approaching the transition reforms that took place in

Romanian agriculture after 1989 from the perspective of more than a century of experiments in agricultural policy-making. It will be argued that the post-1989 reforms did not represent totally new policy experiments. In fact, they have been preceded in Romania by three other major periods of agrarian reform-policies: A first wave of policies between 1864 and 1921, followed by another one from 1921 to 1945 (which for convenience will be both referred to as the pre-communist period) and the 1945–1989 policy period which we will refer to as the communist period (or the period of planned agriculture).

During both the pre-communist and communist periods, the Romanian policy makers struggled to define and redefine the core models and strategies that would put an end to the social and economic backwardness specific to an economic dualism prone, agrarian country like Romania. Their policy solutions were very diverse and as one would expect they often diverged. This diversity was contingent upon the historical context in which the policies were implemented, the currents of thought to which the policy makers were attached by education or chance, and last but not least, by the extent to which the free circulation of ideas was accepted under different political regimes. From this standpoint, the pre-communist period had a much more diverse intellectual elite that debated often from opposing theoretical standpoints what needed to be done or what was possible to do in order to escape backwardness (Love, 1998).

By contrast, the communist period was much more homogenous in terms of ideas about development in general and the role of agriculture in development in particular. It was also a period in which policy choices were confined by strict ideological parameters. Nevertheless, a limited participation in the circulation of ideas about development, as defined or filtered in the Soviet Union's space of influence was possible. The Council for Mutual Economic Assistance (CMEA also known as Comecon) contributed to the diffusion of these ideas among the member countries.

The abandonment of planned agriculture after 1989 opened up the possibility for a renewed interest in the ideas, theories and paradigms of development and the role of agriculture in the Romanian economic and social context. Moreover, the period represented a major opportunity window for a strategic shift in agrarian policy, of the sort that are "few and far between", free of ideological limitations and unconstrained by the Communist Party's hegemony of action. In this context it makes sense to ask the following question: To what extent the post 1989 agrarian reforms have been influenced by the policy experiences of the previous periods? More specifically, can we speak of a policy learning process in the post 1989 agrarian reforms? Did, as authors such as Tomich, Kilby, and Johnson (1995) would expect, the "catastrophic learning experiences" of the past, force the leading ideas or strategic notions to change in the new context? Were the policymakers able to set adequate priorities and sort through the abundance of possible strategic notions so as to match the historical opportunity window with the right policies? Put otherwise, is it possible to tentatively evaluate the effect of ideas, in the narrowly defined sense of causal beliefs (or beliefs about cause-effect relationship), on the agrarian reforms of the post-1989 period?

Before proceeding to an overview of the structure of the study, a brief further note on the definition of "rational" policy-making in which standard learning processes are operating needs to be made. To make things clearer, let us use a strong definition of policy-making rationality, by which we mean that a rational policy process necessarily incorporates some key concepts and ideas (i.e. reflects a prior process of descriptive inferences) that are linked by a causal mechanism or set of causal inferences, which are informed and formed on the basis of past experiences. Moreover, policy-making is a *strategically* oriented process, that is, the rationality of policy-making depends on both the rationality of the goal to be reached and of the process/mechanism by which the goal is achieved. In other words, the core of policy-making, rationality is embodied ultimately as a *learning process*.

Implicit in this definition is a concentric view of rationality with a core defined in terms of ideas about causal relationships and an external belt or periphery sensitive to other strategic considerations related to interest groups, structural constraints, and historical contingencies. In spite of the fact that when investigating the case, the strong definition of policy-making rationality will be used as a benchmark, we are aware that in fact, there is a spectrum of rationality with differences of degree and not of nature. The "external belt" rationality of policy implementation will be abundantly illustrated and instantiated in the following chapters. Our approach agrees with positions such as those formulated by Timmer (1998) arguing that when markets are not the sole resource distributers—and in development processes they often are not—and when policy makers intervene in the process of resource allocation, ideas start to matter because the framework of constraints and objectives in which the policy makers' act is itself "ultimately conditioned by the prevailing academic understanding of how economic growth proceeds" (1998: 115).

At this point, let us briefly add a methodological corollary. Given that nearly everyone in the field of social sciences agrees that nearly everything "matters" to some extent, (including "ideas" or "policy paradigms") the real problem is to determine how ideas matter in the specific case in point and hopefully in the class of similar cases. The most fundamental point that should be recognized in this respect is that a search for a universal account of the causal weight assigned to ideas is not a very promising research venue. Indeed, research on this line makes sense only in the context of a specific process tracing and careful contextual and configurational analysis over very concrete historical situations and cases, reinforced sometimes by counterfactual analysis. This is the sole meaningful way to engage into the clarification of such causal claims.

The epistemological implication of this reality is that the approach to the role of ideas assumed here is an attempt to equilibrate different methodologies and to develop a pluralistic perspective that rejects simple notions of causality and reductionist explanations. The students of ideas must engage in attempts of *verstehen*, the interpretation of meaning through empathetic understanding and by the exploration of actions and artifacts embodying and reflecting those ideas. As a consequence, such projects have to reconcile the demand for systematic social science with the recognition of the role of interpretation and adopt a method of inquiry that combines both description and causal inference (Haas, 1990: 9; King, Keohane, & Verba, 1994).

Returning from the methodological excursion to the underlying framework behind the project, it has already been mentioned that in the hypothesis of a rational policy making process and under the definition of "rationality" given above, the post 1989 agricultural reforms should have been informed by the lessons provided by both the pre-communist and communist periods. The implication of this conjecture is rather straightforward: It requires first to identify the main sequences of ideas—policies—results—lessons that characterized each of the pre-communist, communist, and post-communist periods. Second, it intimates a comparison of the ideas, policies, and lessons that could have been drawn from past experiences in regard to agricultural development with the actual ideas and agricultural policies that have been implemented in the post-communist period. Such comparison—be it implicit or explicit—could reveal the extent to which learning and hence the rational decision-making model was at work or not.

All of the above are the basic building blocks framing the approach and the structure of the book. Given this underlying framework, the book will proceed along the following lines:

The key post-communist legislation regarding agriculture that was passed from 1989 to about 2000, prior to the major thrust reorienting Romania's national strategy towards the EU accession, will be identified. By the detailed analysis of this corpus of legislation and of one of the most comprehensive reports on agriculture issued by the Ministry of Agriculture and Food in Romania in 1999–2000, the dominant agricultural policy paradigm of the period, the key ideas that were behind it, and the main consequences that followed for agriculture will be pinpointed. The major agricultural reform policies in the pre-communist and communist periods (1864–1948 and 1948–1989) and the basic concepts and theories that informed each of them will be documented. Thereafter, an overview of the economic, sociological and structural consequences of these ideas and policies will be provided and some main insights that could be eventually derived by looking in retrospect to each of the periods will be outlined.

In accordance with these objectives, the study proceeds as follows. After introducing in Chap. 3 dualism as the background on which the policy reforms discussed in the book are unfolding and after presenting it as a structural constraint on any policy idea or initiative, in Chap. 4 we overview the Romanian reform legislation between 1989 and 2000. In line with the logic and approach introduced above, we use this legislation as a vehicle to reveal the key ideas, policies and consequences for agricultural development in the last, post-communist decade. Chapters 4 and 5 add the second dimension of the study. More precisely, in Chap. 5 we start by looking at the policy reforms in the pre-communist period, while in parallel outlining the main ideas, policies, consequences, and lessons of the period. Similarly, in Chap. 6 we describe the main policy reforms of the communist period and we pay special attention to the lessons that could have been drawn from this period's policies and their consequences. In the *conclusions* chapter we wrap up the analysis and we put the pieces together in a comparative, systematic way focusing on the sequence ideas—policies—results—lessons. Last but not least, we derive some tentative conclusions regarding the multiple dimensions of the study and its relevance not only for the study of public policy and structural reform strategies but also for the study of Romanian economic history or the analysis of societies and economies whose development and modernization is defined by the structural constraints of dualism.

References

Haas, E. B. (1990). *When knowledge is power: Three models of change in international organizations*. Berkeley, CA: University of California Press.

Hall, P. A. (Ed.). (1989). *The political power of economic ideas: Keynesianism across nations*. Princeton, NJ: Princeton University Press.

King, G., Keohane, R. E., & Verba, S. (1994). *Designing social inquiry: Scientific inference in qualitative research*. Princeton, NJ: Princeton University Press.

Love, J. L. (1998). Dependency theories in Rumania before 1945. In J. Batou & T. David (Eds.), *Uneven development in Europe 1918–1939* (pp. 85–106). Geneva: Droz.

Timmer, P. (1998). The agricultural transformation. In C. K. Eicher & J. M. Staatz (Eds.), *International agricultural development* (pp. 113–135). Baltimore, MD: The John Hopkins University Press.

Tomich, T. P., Kilby, P., & Johnson, B. F. (1995). *Transforming agrarian economies. Opportunities seized, opportunities missed*. Ithaca, NY: Cornell University Press.

Chapter 3
Economic Dualism as a Structural Constraint of South Eastern European Economies and Societies

Abstract This chapter introduces the notion of economic and social dualism as a system that comprises a modern economy co-existing with a traditional, oversized peasant economy and the two, while having contact with each other, are not and cannot be fully integrated. The chapter presents dualism as a background on which the book's argument will operate. Then it moves to show how the notion of dualism could be fruitfully applied to the description and analysis of the Eastern European economies and societies. The last part of the chapter focuses on the specific case of Romania, introduced as a particular case of economic dualism necessitating a structural reform of the agricultural sector as a crucial step in the modernization of the country.

Keywords Dual economy · Traditional economy · Economic modernization · Structural reform · Development policies · Industrialization

The concept of "economic dualism" (or of "dual economy") has a rather long intellectual history, and has gained an important place, as key notion in development economics textbooks. The dualism literature was originated in the early twentieth century by J. H. Boeke's studies of economic growth in underdeveloped nations. His main case studies were the European-owned plantations in South East Asia, run along modern capitalist lines but that coexisted with an indigenous agrarian economy where peasants worked and lived along the traditional lines (Boeke, 1953). As already noted, the key insight was that of the existence of a dual economy having advanced and backward sectors which remained distinct and where capitalism operated along with a peasant economy embodying pre-capitalist social values and relationships. The two, while having contact with each other, are not and cannot be fully integrated. The basic implication was that economic laws valid for capitalist societies were not valid for dual economies. Due to its descriptive and explanatory power this basic way of conceptualizing economies and societies was extensively used in development and modernization theory (Gersovitz, 1983; Todaro, 1985).

Indeed, at a closer look, the models of economic development have been—up to a point—dualistic, contrasting a traditional, agricultural, sector with a modern, industrial, sector. The economic development literature argued that different cultural, normative and behavioral patterns characterize the former relative to the latter, and

A. Dabu and P. D. Aligica, *Economic Dualism and Agrarian Policies*,
SpringerBriefs in Economics, https://doi.org/10.1007/978-3-030-47836-0_3

that economic development involves the transfer of resources, broadly defined, to the modem sector. It is in this sector where capital accumulation and productivity growth occur. Thus, development involves a displacement of the traditional sector and its conversion into the modern one.

This theory was later extended from the economy to societies as a whole, and the concept was used for the description of all economies and societies segmented into advanced and backward sectors. From there to its usage to describe any economy that is split into two manifest sectors, irrespective of their nature, was only one step. Indeed, currently the notion of dualism is also applied to more developed economies, where core regions with large-scale, thriving industries compare with their less developed peripheries. Northern Italy and the Mezzogiorno are often quoted as an example but sometimes even the US economy is approached with a dualist lense. The idea is that the notion of dualism has slowly become independent of its development theory roots. Dualism, broadly defined, comes to define a structural feature of an economic or social system characterized by the uneasy coexistence of two major sectors (Averitt, 1968; Casals, 1980).

Irrespective the specific definition used in a context or another, there are two possible dimensions that are implicit in any application of the notion of dualism. The first is a historical dimension conceptualizing the social dynamics of a phenomenon. This dimension is best reflected by the way dualism is employed in development and modernization theories. The evolution of the phenomenon is defined in terms of stages or a sequence of systems and sub-systems, each corresponding to a historical "stage". The moment of coexistence of two systems in the evolution process is a dualist moment. The Boeke, traditional-modern sequence, Rostow's stages of economic growth or the East European neo-Marxist focus on the sequence feudalism-capitalism are a good illustration in this respect (Love, 1996).

The second dimension is a structural one and it offers a refined perspective on the possible facets of dualism. From this perspective, dualism may be described on at least three levels: economic, social and cultural. Indeed, a realist description of the economic system is incomplete without references to the social and cultural element that encapsulate it. Nevertheless, it is important to note that for analytical purposes the three levels may be addressed relatively autonomously. Identifying and isolating its key elements for analytical reasons, is an important contribution to a more profound understanding of dualism. Consequently, economic dualism may retain its analytical potential even when it is conceptually disentangled from its cultural and social context.

For instance, the distinction between traditional and modern sectors can still be maintained, even if one drops all assumptions concerning differences in culture and attitudes. Even if peasant farmers have a "capitalist" mindset and are as interested in economic returns as are industrial entrepreneurs or commercial oriented farmers, the model remains viable. One can argue that modern sectors are those that have moved from *social* exchange, which has existed throughout most of history, to a *market* system and modern forms of socio-economic organization (Grabowski, 1995). The latter is characterized by a social and geographical integration of markets in which there is a tendency to converge toward uniformity and towards modern production and distribution organizational forms. Alternatively, traditional sectors of an economy represent areas where such integration has yet to occur and are still organized on traditional bases (Grabowski, 1995).

The key point is that even if we strip the concept of dualism of its cultural element, the remaining social and economic elements are still powerful enough to offer a viable analytical framework. Moreover, we can take a step even further by putting into parentheses the social element and letting a pure economic model emerge. In fact, that (macro)economic perspective has been the mainstream approach to the problem. In this respect, the work of Lewis probably best represents the traditional models of economic dualism (Gersovitz, 1983). His work presumes the existence of a traditional and modern sector. Lewis maintains that the traditional sector may contain components of both agriculture and manufacturing, as does the modern sector. The real and main distinction between sectors is based upon how resources are allocated, and especially labor or human resources. In the modern sector, labor is hired up to the point where the marginal product equals the wage rate. In the traditional sector, labor is paid according to traditional rules or mechanisms. Usually farming or other activities are conducted on a family basis, with the output being distributed equally among members. Thus, labor in this sector is being paid at its average rather than marginal product. The result is that the traditional sector is plagued with a labor market distortion because the marginal product of labor is thought to be below the average product. Since the marginal product represents the social opportunity cost of labor, *the modern sector will have to pay too high of a wage to attract labor*. It will have to pay a wage at least as high as the average product of labor in the traditional sector. Thus, *too much labor remains in the latter sector and not enough in the modern sector*: The traditional sector is characterized by surplus labor (Gersovitz, 1983; Todaro, 1985). That has serious implications not only for any economic strategy developed by the state but also for the very way the state itself organizes in order to cope with that problem.

Even a superficial overview of the dualism issue, reveals that its existence has been a profound determinant of social, economic and political processes and a source of frictions, tensions and blockages. Nevertheless, dualism is unavoidable for any modernizing or developing country: dualism may be seen in the end as just another face of development. If we adopt the conceptual lenses of the dualist theory, the inevitable answer to the development question is that development occurs as capital accumulation in the modern sector draws labor out of the traditional sector. Therefore, the modern sector is the engine of economic growth, which eventually displaces the traditional sector. Thus, the preeminence of the economic aspect seems to be intuitively clear-cut.

To sum up, in any of its varieties-cultural, social or economic—dualism offers a very powerful analytical and heuristic tool. If used to analyze social change it clearly illuminates with conceptual clarity a set of realities that are intuitively understood by any researcher of development. In addition to that, it creates the possibility to better articulate those intuitions through clearly defined models or theoretical frameworks and to open up the way for consistent conceptually based policy solutions.

3.1 Dualism and South East European Countries

Out of the complex set of social, cultural and economic relationships illuminated by the concept of dualism, the main focus of our argument is on the core economic aspect. Social and cultural dualism are to be regarded—for the purposes of this discussion—only in those aspects that are connected to and may illustrate the impact of economic dualism. Consequently, the operational definition of dualism in South Eastern Europe will be given primarily in basic economic and demographic terms following the traditional approach centered on the rural-urban and agriculture-industry polarity.

Accordingly we are not laying the emphasis on ethnicity, nationalism or religion as the mainstream approaches to the states and problems of the South East European region usually do, but on the regional political economies and on what this book considers to be their key *structural* problem. It is indeed difficult to imagine and analyze the South Eastern Europe problems making abstraction of the powerful ethnic and religious forces that shaped the destiny of the region but it is important to approach these problems from different and complementary angles. The present analysis implies a simplification indeed, but it is an instrumental and pragmatic one that helps us to discern and disentangle some patterns or configurations of factors relevant for a better understanding of the internal evolutions and of the international integration prospects of South Eastern Europe. The main objective is to use a specific way of conceptualizing the political economy dynamics of the region in order to illuminate from a structural and historic perspective a crucial problem currently faced by the states of the region in their attempt to settle on the path of self-sustained growth and full European integration.

It is clear that irrespective their specific definition, the dualist models apply indeed, at one point or another, to all countries during their histories, and the South East European ones were no exception. But while the majority of other European countries went through a transition period of economic dualism, they overcome it and then entered a mature phase of industrial economy the South Eastern Europe countries development and modernization trajectory was deviated by dualism in a specific direction. In the case of the countries that today are called "advanced industrial democracies", dualism was a moment or a stage of economic development. On the other hand, for the South Eastern Europe countries, dualism was a constant and active deterring factor on the development path. That fact was noticed by the pioneers of development theory. In fact, the Balkans and South Eastern Europe were their basic source of inspiration and case study before and immediately after the Second World War (Rosenstein-Rodan, 1959; Love, 1996).

There is no doubt about the fact that South Eastern Europe countries had in the past all the standard features of dualism (Spulber, 1966; Lampe & Jackson, 1982). There was a strong traditional sector centered on agriculture and its absorbing was slow, incomplete, imperfect and inefficient. As "late, late industrialisers", the states of the region had many priorities: political independence, nation building ethnic and geopolitical challenges, basic political and economic institution building etc. and thus in spite of the fact that the dualism of their economic structure was important as a background factor it was only secondary on the agenda.

The complex dualism of South Eastern Europe was evident to all foreign analysts of the region. The typical description of these countries by external observers was very well epitomized by a British diplomat: "In analyzing their national character you have two distinct classes to deal with—the governmental and commercial which wear coats, trousers and boots and the peasant which affect jackets, petticoats and sandals" (Mazover, 2000). The cultural and social dualism was so blatant that it was reducible to pure human typologies. Moreover, for the entire period of modernization there was an open and constant tension between the two sectors, a tension that was clear to all foreign observers of the region. For them, as for all local supporters of modernization, it was evident that peasants tried to resist the incursions of modernity. For centuries the village had been the main political, administrative and economic unit organizing the collective lives of rural inhabitants of Balkans. In the XIX century this isolated collectivity began to change in ways its inhabitants found hard to comprehend. For them money meant exploitation, shops and commerce implied degeneration (Mazover 2000, 33). That affected indeed the political dynamics of the modern states of the region.

Acknowledging the fact that development occurs as capital accumulation in the modern sector draws labor out of the traditional sector, and recognizing the crucial role of agriculture in facilitating or impeding this process, modern states used their economic policy leverage to achieve that goal by repeatedly trying to reform agriculture. The problem was that in practice things were not so easy. There were many complications that hindered the process of displacement, starting from economic one, like the terms of trade and ending with cultural ones, like dysfunctional persistence of traditional values and resistance to change. The entire political system was affected by dualism, too. It is therefore not surprising that states were not only the subjects of pressures generated by dualism but also inevitably took an active role in acting against it. States had to envisage policies responding to and dealing with these problems at all levels and on a large set of issue areas (Mitrany, 1951).

The problem was that no decisive solution was found to the "agrarian challenge" facing the new South Eastern Europe states. The attempt to solve the problem through the land reforms in the 1920s was far from successful. The new land distribution neither generated the modernization of the sector nor guaranteed peasants a living (Mitrany, 1951; Spulber, 1966; Lampe & Jackson, 1982; Jelavich & Jelavich, 1974); On the contrary, the result was more fragmentation and more inefficiency. These reforms led to a notable rise in small subsistence farming, accounting for at least two-thirds of the landholdings and for at least one-third of the cultivated land. Almost 80% of the labor force of Romania, Yugoslavia, and Bulgaria remained engaged in agriculture while in Greece, a country heavily dependent on trade and sea shipping, it reached about 50%. Given the rapid rate of increase in population and in the labor force and, given the limited capacity of labor intake in industry, increasing pressures on land was accumulating in the countryside (Lampe & Jackson, 1982; Spulber, 1966, 60–74). The efforts made to expand the cultivated area and the yields were not very successful and even in their success they tended to reinforce the base of the traditional sector. During that period the area was expanded by 10–20% in Romania, Yugoslavia and Bulgaria, and by as much as 70% in Greece (where about only one-fourth of the surface of the country is cultivable). In spite of these increases, per-capita productivity remained exceptionally low. Furthermore, the limited output increases were facing an over-all growth in population of 25–30% (Spulber, 1966, 69–72). And although the largest part of the population was dependent on agriculture, and even though agricultural output might have been increased significantly by improving farming methods little was done to support the real modernization of this sector. Except in Greece, "where the influx of refugees forced the government to turn its attention to agriculture, in the rest of the area the governments failed to focus in a positive way on this sector either directly or indirectly" (Spulber, 1966, 71).

The reasons for this situation were the result of a blend between the incentives given by the international economy by that time and a specific vision on the modernization strategy centered around industry and industrialization:

> As a result of a falling demand for agricultural produce on the world markets and with the drives toward self-sufficiency of the advanced countries (and on the other hand, incapable either to stop the process of splitting up of land-holdings in agriculture or of reducing the demographic pressures), the governments of the area turned their hopes toward industrialization and toward wider state intervention in the economy. As usually happens, however, sharp differences arose about what course industrialization should take. The agrarian parties confusedly aimed at the development of competitive industries close to agriculture and exposed any other policy as a devious plan of "monopoly capitalism." The other parties aimed at developing fully integrated industrial complexes within each national entity without regard to actual factor endowment. (Spulber, 1966, 72)

The depression of the 1930s increased even more the drive toward self-sufficiency. An entire set of measures with erroneous fiscal, monetary, and lending policies meant to encourage national industry was enacted in total disregard for the balance between the sectors and the equilibrium of the economy. Thus, there is no surprise that by the end of the period the progress was dim, and the structural problem of the economy was looming large behind the optimistic industrial production increases statistics. The data on the population employed in agriculture and the traditional sector before the Second World War offer a clear and grim view. By that time the percentage of population employed in the traditional sector was 80% in Bulgaria, 75% in Greece, 77% in Romania, 80% in Turkey and 78% in Yugoslavia while the percentage of national product from agriculture (usually including forestry and fisheries) was 40% in Bulgaria, 40% in Greece, 45% in Romania, 50% in Turkey, and 40% in Yugoslavia (Mitchell, 1998).

The same percentages pretty much describe the situation at the beginning of the Cold War. During the Cold War the countries of the region took on different paths: while Turkey and Greece had some continuity with their ante-war policies (and at one point Greece fully benefited of the European Integration process), in the rest of the region a forced industrialization program was imposed in various forms and degrees as a solution by the communist regimes. But this type of industrialization only apparently solved the problem. In fact, it is safe to conjecture that it complicated the problems even more. All communist countries were forced to reproduce in miniature the Soviet economy. Moreover, at one point, communism became even further hyper-nationalistic than interwar nationalists. All these countries, "including Yugoslavia—which broke away from Soviet dogma in many respects but not in this one—started to channel most of their investments to industry" (Spulber 1966, 73). That materialized at the level of strategy in the attempt to impose a given pattern of investment and a sustained effort of developing within each national entity a whole set of new industries without any consideration for economic rationality. Thus after the collapse of communism, it is tempting to consider that the economies and societies of the region were challenged by a "double dualism": on the one hand a modern sector versus a traditional sector (or at least surviving fragments of it) and on the other hand a (post)communist sector versus a market sector.

Given this background, there are a series of questions that could and should be raised regarding this particular feature of the region: First and most important is whether the South East European societies and economies could still be described as dualist: Is the region still ridded by dualism? Then there are other issues deserving a careful consideration: Did the communist economic structures created by forced industrialization generate a new type of dualism in the relevant countries of the region in the light of the economic reform process? If dualism is not anymore a proper way of describing these societies, then are there any path dependent processes and features that survived and that are still influencing the state of the political system? In what measure are the cleavages and the organized interest in the region shaped by dualist structures? What is the relationship between traditional dualist structures and the informal economy? Is governance under dualist conditions different from governance in advanced industrial democracies? If yes, in what measure are the governance models imported from the latter viable? What are the implications of dualism for the future of the region and the dynamics globalization in that part of the world?

3.2 Dualism in the Balkans: Exploratory Overview of Some Implications

It is obvious that all these questions make up for an entire research program beyond the limits of the present book. The book will focus only on one limited set of issues, pertaining to the problem of the policy reforms meant to address the structural constraints of dualism and to the ideas inspiring those policies. However, it is still possible within the limits of this chapter, to offer a starting point for dealing with some the abovementioned questions. One could do that by following several of the implications of dualism in a number of the issue-areas that have been and will continue to be extremely relevant for the dynamics of the states of the region and for the region as a whole. The basic tenet of the rest of the discussion is that the answer to the basic question is either a strong: "Yes, dualism is still a viable way of approaching and understanding the South Eastern European societies" or (at least) a weaker variant:

"Dualism as such is fading away but its legacies and implications continue to be relevant".

A cursory overview of relevant data supports at least the weak thesis: even now the agricultural sector (a good indicator for the size of the traditional sector as percent of the population and GDP) (Gersovitz, 1983; Todaro, 1985) is extremely large: the regional average is 40%. Also the rural-urban balance is still tilted towards the rural in comparison to other European states while as the statistics show the efficiency and productivity of the agricultural sector is low and not reflected in the exports of the countries (a sign of the existing large disequilibrium between the primary sector and the other sectors). The percentage of the employment in agriculture and of the rural population for the 1990–2000 decade remains very high on all standards in each country of the region: Albania (58%, 61%); Bosnia and Herzegovina (32%, 59%); Bulgaria (35%, 32%); Croatia (17%, 44%); Greece (34%, 41%); Republic of Moldova (43%, 54%); Romania (38%, 45%); Slovenia (17%, 50%); the former Yugoslavian Republic of Macedonia (40%, 40%), Turkey (65%, 31%); and Yugoslavia (Serbia/Montenegro) with the agricultural employment unavailable and the rural population at about 50% (World Bank, 2001).

If we compare the percentage of the employment in agriculture and of the rural population with the available statistics on the structure of gross value added, the structural tension in the economies of the region is even clearer. The regional average was, around the turn of the century, 15% gross value added from agriculture, 25% from industry, 5% from constructions and 50% from services (European Commission, 2001). The fact that overall in the region roughly 40% of the GDP is produced in a sector that has a gross value added of about 15% is a telling indicator of the productivity of that sector and of its degree of technological and organizational modernization. That conclusion could be augmented by the fact that low-tech mining and extractive industries represent with a large variance (mainly due to Greece) on the average 50% of the industrial gross value added. Various indicators regarding the geographical distribution of population and the degree of penetration of modern communication technologies are further evidence of the yet significant dualism of the region. The largest urban agglomerations in each country of the region represent on the average 20% of the total of urban population and around 10% of the total population. The exception is again Greece which 51% of its urban population and 30% of the total population in Athens (United Nations, 1997). South Eastern Europe seems a region that is still strongly divided on the rural/urban line. The regional standards of living and quality of life tell a similar story, an estimated 60% of the rural households having no running water and a limited direct access to health care even in countries like Romania that did not suffer from the disruptions of war (Research Institute for the Quality of Life, 2000).

If we accept the idea of the constant presence of a dualist factor determining the social and economic evolution of the region, then we could take a structural and long run view at several questions pertaining to key areas of the domestic social and political system. In the light of this effort focused on domestic structures, we shall be able to approach in the end in a fresh way the situation of South Eastern Europe in the European and global context.

First, it should be noted that dualism has strong implications for the political culture of the South Eastern Europe states. From a cultural standpoint, the existence of dualism implies the existence of an important segment of population with a specific traditional cultural and behavioral pattern. It is expected that in the region, the values associated to the traditional societies and cultures are much more present, will continue to be and that this reality will imply a tacit but significant resistance to change in the political culture of the countries of the region (Tismaneanu, 1995). That, as it has been extensively documented in the literature, could take specific political culture forms: collectivism, authoritarianism, animosity to individual rights and to ethnic and religious diversity and differences (Tismaneanu, 1998). Moreover, there is a strong correlation between those cultural traits and a nationalist political culture. Consequently, the raise of nationalism in the aftermath of the communist collapse shouldn't have been a surprise (Sugar and Lederer, 1994; Tismaneanu, 1998; Verdery, 1995).

In the context of a discussion that pivots on the issue of economic dualism, it is important to stress the fact that in South Eastern Europe political culture was *reinforced by a specific economic background*, in other words it was not floating freely at the margin of the modern system in a state of amorphous anomy. Neither the people are simply resistant to change due to pure irrational attachments to specific values (Tismaneanu, 1995; Islam, 2001). Culture in itself may not be very potent. Its strengths may come when it is anchored in a specific economic and institutional structure that reinforces it (Tismaneanu, 1995). And in the case of South Eastern Europe, economic dualism is one of the deepest and most important structural forces that shape the attitudes and values of the people of the region (Verdery, 1995; Tismaneanu, 1995).

Therefore, in the measure in which political culture has been a problem for the development of the region it is important to note that it will be more likely to be changed by structural transformations in the economy than by propaganda or by "cultural politics" campaigns. As we'll illustrate in the next chapters, the resilience of culture was tested by the communists' attempt towards such a transformation. The communist experience is very troubling as its experiment in social change was in fact focused both on education campaigns and on structural changes (industrialization) (Verdery, 1995). In the current research on the impact of traditional culture on political and economic dynamics in South Eastern Europe enough evidence has been accumulated to document the economic roots of the resilience of cultural traditionalism in the region (Burawoy and Verdery, 1999).

A similar argument could be made regarding the relationship between economic and social dualism. The key issue in this respect is that traditional societies are social exchange societies. The interpersonal social networks are one of their key features and their strengths might explain the resilience of dualism. In a dualist system, social exchange networks penetrate the entire society, including the modern sector. If market relations do not connect the traditional sector to the modern one, social networks do. But they do more than that, they penetrate the modern sector and affect its structure and functioning. The stronger the traditional sector, the stronger the penetration. That is the reason why the ratios urban/rural, agriculture/industry used above as descriptive indicators, are not an entirely accurate statistic of the strengths of the traditional sector. Political society has its share of such penetration too. Moreover, the system of patronage and cronyism, as mechanisms of linking the sectors, may become a defining feature of the political society in dualist countries. In the case of the South Eastern Europe countries the perception is that this is precisely the case. Specific relationships, irrespective the way we call them (family, clan, group etc.) are interfering with the modern structures and the functioning of the formal institutions. Corruption is one of the outcomes but not the sole (Minassian, 2002; Recanatini & Broadman, 2001). In this respect, it is interesting to quote an insightful analyst of the region that noted that after the 1950s:

> Peasants moved away from the countryside and brought up children who went to school, developed new conceptions of consumption and leisure and earned enough money to take vacations by the Black Sea, the Adriatic or the Aegean. On the other hand, peasants retained their attachment to the village and soil even after moving into towns and changing their patterns of life (…) Villages still supplied fresh food, pigs and fruit more reliably and cheaply than the officially rationed distribution and retail system. Social networks were transplanted from the village or family into government the army and the economy. In other words, urbanization often meant the village being brought into the city. And perhaps in some ways taking it over too: the personalized interactions gifts and favors which lubricated dealings with state officialdom could be misinterpreted by the unaware as forms of "corruption" rather than a natural response to the impersonal mechanism of modern government. (Mazover, 2000, 136)

The coexistence of strong traditional ties, based on rural settlements, reinforced by the ongoing engagement in traditional economic activities and defined by traditional cultural values and norms, represents a significant factor determining the socio-political dynamics of the region (Metzo, 1999). Again, in this case as well, preaching or legalistic, anti-corruption campaigns lead by the government are of little effect as long the dualist economic structure subsides. As long it is more effective to use social exchange networks instead of market ones, stopping the phenomenon is unlikely. Only the reduction of the traditional sector is a minimal guarantee of success, a necessary but not sufficient condition. Even so an inertial and path dependent trend might continue for some time (Burawoy & Verdery, 1999). Thus one solution seems to be a deliberate attempt by the state to establish market systems, as opposed to social exchange ones; in other words, to penetrate and to destroy the social networks by market networks. Also, it should be noted that marketization seems also to be the sole long-term viable solution for re-channeling and neutralizing the impact of ethnic and religious networks, ties and influence groups (Jones, Hellman and Kaufmann, 2001).

In connection to that, it is important to also note the existence of cleavages created on the dualist basis, besides the better-known and studied ones—i.e. the ethnic and religious. It is conceivable that the tensions generated by dualism are translated and transferred by the population in ethnic and religious terms, although that conjecture remains to be explored. Sometimes the modern or developed areas coincide with the ethnic or religious ones but such situation is not typical. This structural cleavage, not obvious but always present, might be of more explanatory and policy importance than we think.

Conceptualizing the South Eastern European situation in terms of dualism leads to the idea that during their modern history the states from the region had to accommodate the political groups, movements and forces coming from the two different sectors. States had to behave in modern ways but with political forces and movements that had traditional bases. Moreover these forces manifested (and in some countries continue to manifest) themselves in coalitions, parties and political movements that didn't want only to take control of the state but also to change the very nature of the state. The traditional sector generated movements and coalitions that had a basic uneasiness with specific features of the modern state in itself and not with this or that specific or minor institutional aspect or organizational form (Roucek, 1939).

To sum up, economic dualism represents an anchor for social and cultural dualism. Together the three generate a reinforcing system that has significant direct and spillover effects on the political economy system and on the policies of the states of the region. They fuel collectivistic and authoritarian political culture; reinforce political nationalism and encourage its political use by elites, generates cleavages that profoundly affect the politics and policies of the region and shape the economic and social policies of the states through interest groups and political pressure. Probably the best illustrations of these factors at work are the populist movements and the specific difficulties affecting the role of the state in economic policies in the region.

It is noteworthy that the literature agrees that the main tension in the region, and its main cleavage was not between a socialist/revolutionary/Marxist left and a liberal conservative capitalist right but between a populist (usually an Agrarian) traditionalist movement and the pro-modernization political coalitions (Mitrany, 1951). This has special implications for the way political parties, movements and organized interests should be perceived in the region. Historically, agrarian populism was the main form of political reaction of the traditional sector: it opposed the urban centers, urbanization tendencies and capitalism (Held, 1996). Quite unsurprisingly on its positive agenda was the creation/preservation of small family holdings, sometimes the founding of cooperatives and strengthening of the communities, and a self-governance ideology in which the peasant was considered to be the source of morality and agricultural life the basis of society (Held, 1996; Ionescu, 1969, 97–121). Initially in Eastern Europe due to its very social and cultural nature, and to the existing infrastructure, agrarian populist movements were unable to influence politics at the national level. The first movements were mainly regional and had a high violence potential in the sense that they easily involved clashes with the government authority.

Later in the twentieth century, in most East European countries populism in its agrarian form became a powerful force of political organized interests and source of legitimacy for them. In a region where peasants and other traditional sector related people constituted the large majority of the population, agrarian populism soon became one of (if not) the dominant political trend(s). The more the modernization process stepped up the more the traditionalist-agrarian populism increased in influence. These movements were very diverse but all had in common a very strong anti-capitalist and anti-liberal attitude and rhetoric. Moreover, in many cases they took a nationalist dimension by associating capitalism and liberalism with alien nations or people. Modern institutions and capitalism were seen as an alien element forcefully imposed to East European societies by alien or anti-national elites.

Populist agrarian parties had a significant advance through electoral victories in the early twentieth century but their governments were generally short-lived (Held, 1996; Ionescu 1969, 97–121). When the communists took power after World War II, peasant organizations were either forcefully integrated into the ruling Communist Party or co-opted as so-called "bloc" or "satellite" parties (Pryor, 1992). Later, and especially in the final period of the regime, tradition-oriented populism was used during communism as part of the official ideological mix that included nationalism and socialism (Verdery, 1995; Jelavich, 1983). After the fall of communism, not only that peasant parties reappeared in all East European countries but populism reasserted itself as a powerful force. Rural areas in many post-communist countries form the backbone of communist successor parties that continue to build up on the ideological mix they cooked up in the 1980' (Held, 1996; Crampton, 2002). To sum up, the basic point is that populism (and in general agrarian populism with traditionalist and nationalist tones) is an invariable in South Eastern European politics and this is one of the key symptoms of a strong dualist legacy.

The second area where the impact of dualism is clearly illustrated is the South Eastern European states' economic policy. It is clear that the states in dual economies and societies are in an uneasy position not only politically but also financially. That has always seemed to be the case with the South Eastern European states (Lampe & Jackson, 1982; Jelavich and Jelavich, 1974; Jelavich, 1983). During their entire history they had to link, mediate and balance the two sectors while trying to undermine and diminish one of them (make the traditional to be absorbed by the modern). This was not an easy policy task and required huge state efforts and many of their limited resources were used by it. Moreover as long as dualism and its legacies has continues to exist, the South Eastern European states have had to allocate resources between the two systems in a strategic or planned way. Taxation has become thus a special problem. The standard approach to the problem was squeezing the traditional sector for the benefit of the modern, a fact that definitely contributed to the increase of the tensions between the two. Therefore as long that dualism exists, the South Eastern European states are forced to react in many and sometimes contradictory ways and create peculiar political economic institutional arrangements both to accommodate the continuous existence of the traditional sector and to try to economically and politically undermine and absorb it into the modern one at the same time. The problem gains a new dimension when the pressure put by globalization is filtered in a democratic system in which the traditional sector may amplify those pressures through the parliamentary channels.

The crucial question to be asked regarding the states' strategy in this respect is in what measure the *industrialization* solution of the dualist problem was/is the right strategy. The typical approach advocated and implemented before the Second World War was to place emphasis on industry and the creation of an industrial basis. As it has been established by the literature, the communists were not innovators: in the states where they took control, they simply ruthlessly pushed the industrialization process already promoted by the previous regime in a "forced" industrialization direction (Spulber, 1966).

The problem that needs to be emphasized as regarding the industrialization-centered strategy is the misleading association of modernity directly with industry and its policy consequence. Structuring the states' strategy based on this understanding was in no way a success. Industrialization seems in many respects as more of an externality, a secondary outcome of a deeper process. The key may not be the transfer of resources from the traditional to the modern sector (that is defined in industrial terms). Instead, it may be that the transformation of a *social* exchange system to a *market* system is the surest mark of economic development and modernization. Industrialization may be an outcome of the process, not the means of achieving it. Further, in the case of South Eastern European countries, the traditional sector is overwhelmingly agricultural, and thus development should have involved the creation of a market economy within this sector. In fact, based on all we know today, marketization seems to be an essential condition for the eventual development of modern industry (Grabowski, 1995).

Thus, the conclusions of a brief overview of the impact of dualism on state lead economic policies raises very important questions. The truth is that the *establishment* of market systems has, however, received far less attention from the economists than the analysis of the *operation* of such systems. Moreover, the problem of marketization in the dualist agrarian South Eastern European has been until recently very low on the agenda. Systems of property rights and enforcement mechanisms for such rights must be established indeed, but these alone are not enough. Viable market relationships between buyers and sellers can survive and expand only if formal rules are reinforced by systems of informal rules. The continuous interaction of the participants in the marketplace in itself is topical in this respect. In this process, the state has a particularly important role to play not so much in terms of creating and disseminating systems of informal rules but in terms of creating an environment in which formal and informal sets of market rules can develop.

All these problems have serious consequences for the policies of the South Eastern European states on their way towards modernization and global and European integration. In a dualist framework it is conceivable that the modern sector fully integrates in the global economy while the traditional one remains behind creating deep pockets of poverty, backwardness and resentment ready to inflame political movements, coalitions and hostile reactions. The deliberate neglect and marginalization of traditional sector in the national or global economy with the hope that it will slowly and painlessly vanish by itself, has serious costs and presents serious dangers.

To sum up, introducing the theme of dualism—with an emphasis of the South Eastern European context—as a background to our discussion, offers a powerful way of framing the Romanian case. Dualism, especially when one of its elements is of a traditional-agrarian nature, is a major determinant of any realistic analysis and theorizing of the social and economic reality defined by it. Moreover, in practical terms, dualism is not a pure internal problem of the states riddled by it or that bear its legacies. The problems and dysfunctions it may create have not only a domestic dimension but also a severe international one. The problem faced by the

Romanian economy and the crucial role agricultural reform policies had to have in the context of its modernization strategies, emerge with clarity in the light of the dualism theory perspective. We have seen that a lot is at stake in any society or economy in which dualism is a structural feature. The solution has unavoidably to deal with the problem of agricultural reform. Irrespective of the approach taken, the problem of the place and role of agriculture in the structure of the economy looms large. In such circumstances, policies aiming at agrarian reform are more than just sectorial policies; they are structural reform policies of national strategic importance.

Once the problem of dualism as a background has been put in place, the stage is set, and we could move now to an in-depth analysis of the Romanian case, a case in which, as one may expect, the problem of the agrarian sector has been on the frontstage since the beginning of the modernization process. In preparation of the in-depth discussion let us briefly overview the basics of the Romanian case in this respect.

3.3 The Romanian Case

Romania's evolution could be described as a process of *late development* in a country in which—for most of its modern history—agriculture represented the most important sector in terms of employed population and for a long while the main contributor to the GDP. At the turn of the century, 36.8% of the active labor force was still employed in agriculture, while 45% (data includes fishing and forestry) of the population lived in rural areas, according to the Romanian Statistical Yearbook. However, agriculture's contribution to the GDP was of 18.8% according to The Economist Intelligence Unit.

The evolution of what was called the Agrarian Problem (*chestiunea agrara*) in Romania consists of four major periods: (1) 1864–1921, (2) 1921–1945, (3) 1945–1989, and (4) after 1989. The fourth one may be divided in two sub-periods with the dividing line given by how one defined the turning point in the process of accession—the moment when the policies, strategies the general social dynamics of the country have turned towards the EU crossing an invisible but massively consequential threshold. As already noted, in the case of this study this point is considered as marked by the year 2000.

This periodization corresponds to key shifting points in the history of agrarian reforms in Romania. In the classic *The Land and the Peasant in Romania* (1968), David Mitrany outlines the main land laws that had been enacted in Romania in the period of 1864–1917 and their socio-economic consequences. The first land redistribution for the peasants in 1864 marked the beginning of the end of pre-modern relationships in agriculture and opened the new era of the peasants' emancipation. However, this first major redistribution of land from the large landlords (*boieri*) toward the peasants was largely incomplete and had many negative, partly unforeseeable consequences for the peasantry. Several other successive land reforms were tried during this first period under the threat of peasants' revolts, the influence of progressive intellectuals (often boyars themselves) or under the pressure of international events such as the First World War.

The inter-war period, analyzed in detail by Henry Roberts' classic study *Rumania—Political Problems of an Agrarian State* (1951), featured a variety of industrial and agrarian policies aimed to boost the modernization of the country. Regarding agriculture, the period started with the second major land redistribution toward the peasants in Romanian history, introduced through the Agrarian Reform Laws of 1921 at the end of the First World War. In general, from a political point of view, the entire period was largely unstable, with several cabinets succeeding each other for short periods of time and with two distinct dictatorial regimes—the King Carol II[1] dictatorship (1938–1940) followed by the Ion Antonescu's dictatorship (1940–1944). However, in spite of the internal and international political and economic instability, several agrarian reforms were enacted and the number of studies on the rural sector problems grew both in number and quality revealing the awareness of the Romanian policy makers and social scientists in respect to the importance of agriculture's modernization for the country's overall development (Roberts, 1951; Love, 1996).

As everywhere else in the Central and East European countries, the post-war era begun in the Romanian agriculture with a new land reform initiated in 1945, at the end of WWII, by the first communist regime in the country's history—the Groza government. It resulted in an extremely fragmented land structure, with holdings of less than 5 ha constituting roughly 75% of all holdings of arable land (Brooks & Meurs, 1994). Albeit conducted by a Communist government, this land reform resembled rather the policy solutions tried in the inter-war period. However, the main aim of the reform was to gain the initial support of the peasants for the Communists (Mitrany, 1951; Roberts, 1951). It was followed only four years later by forced collectivization—this time distinctively shaped by the Communist policy paradigm for agriculture.

In Romania the process of agricultural collectivization began in 1948–49 and was concluded by the early 1960s. Until the beginning of the 1960s, the main goal of the agrarian policies was to consolidate the collective and state farms and to break down the resistance of the peasants toward collectivization. Once collectivization was completed, during the 1960s and 1970s several attempts to better integrate the agricultural and industrial sectors of the economy were made. These attempts were more or less simultaneously introduced in all the Eastern block countries, which were now reunited by the Council for Mutual Economic Assistance (CMEA) created in 1949. The most important agrarian reform strategy adopted by the CMEA countries at the end of the 1960s and during the 1970s was referred to as the "industrialization of agriculture". It consisted practically in the creation of large "agro-industrial complexes" (AIC) on the model of Western agribusiness (Wädekin, 1982). The intention was to integrate agriculture with the rest of the economy by creating clearly defined backward and forward institutional linkages to the rural cooperatives and state farms.

[1] King Carol II reigned from 1930 to 1940.

The expectation was that this process of "vertical integration" would solve the multiple disequilibria problems between industry and agriculture (Wädekin, 1982; Pryor, 1992). Overall, the performance of agriculture remained low, the different organizational solutions advanced by the Romanian communist policy-makers failing to enhance peasants' motivation or to better coordinate the relationship among various sectors of the economy.

The land reform that followed the changes of 1989 was based on the principle of restitution. It was backed by the Law on Land Resources passed in February 1991 and by the Law of Leasing of Agricultural Land passed two years later. Being based on the principle of restitution, it resulted in the reproduction of the extreme fragmentation that characterized the Romanian agriculture before collectivization. During the 1990s, the markets for land, capital and rural labor began to develop but the process was rather slow, given the lack of clear reform programs for agriculture (M. Jackson, 1997). Also the distribution of property titles for land introduced by the 1991 Law on Land Resources was extremely slow (NPADR, 1999). This situation influenced negatively the emergence of land and rural credit markets and the peasants continued to work in informal association, rather than to run individually private farms. An agricultural country Romania did not escape that sociological and economic condition in spite of systematic efforts made during the last century. At the beginning of the new millennium and at the threshold of the EU accession process, many of the structural problems it confronted in the pre-communist or communist periods resurfaced.

To sum up, a constant array of agricultural problems were the object of four major approaches or policy phases during Romanian history. This repeated exercise in policy experiments regarding the very structure of the economy, an exercise that unfolded over a long period of time, offered an excellent setting for policy learning. Thus, besides the interest in its remarkable evolution, the Romanian situation offers the framework for a case study approach of the issue of structural change policies and policy learning. The relatively large number of policy attempts to solve the structural problems in agriculture and the existence of several clearly-cut historical turning points, give Romania the status of a very interesting case study in this respect. The rest of the book will discuss this case in-depth, while at the same time taking it as a vehicle for an exploratory investigation of the relationship between policy reform ideas and structural economic change in countries defined by a dualist structure.

References

Averitt, R. T. (1968). *The dual economy*. New York.

Boeke, J. H. (1953). *Economics and economic policy of dual societies, as exemplified by Indonesia*. New York, NY: International Secretariat, Institute of Pacific Relations.

Brooks, K., & Meurs, M. (1994). Romanian land reform: 1991–1993. *Comparative Economic Studies, 36*(2), 17–32.

Burawoy, M., & Verdery, K. (1999). *Uncertain transition: Ethnographies of change in the postsocialist world*. Lanham, MD: Rowman & Littlefield.

Casals, F. G. (1980). *The syncretic society*. White Plains, NY: M. E. Sharpe.
Crampton, R. J. (2002). *The Balkans since the second world war*. New York, NY: Longman.
Department for Economic and Social Information and Policy Analysis, Statistics Division. (1997). United Nations. *Statistical Yearbook*. New York, NY: United Nations.
Gersovitz, M. (1983). *Selected economic writings of W. Arthur Lewis*. New York: New York University Press.
Grabowski, Richard J. (1995). Economic development and the rise of market systems. *Studies in Comparative International Development, 30*(3), 49–69.
Held, J. (1996). *Populism in Eastern Europe. Racism, nationalism, and society*. Boulder: East European Monographs.
Ionescu, G. (1969). "Eastern Europe" in *Populism. Its meanings and national characteristics*. In: G. Ionescu & E. Gellner (Eds.). London: Weidenfeld and Nicolson.
Islam, R. (2001). *What determines the quality of institutions*? Transition economies working papers. Washington, D.C.: World Bank.
Jackson, M. (1997). Political economy of agricultural reform in Romania. In J. F. M. Swinnen (Ed.), *Political economy of agrarian reform in Central and Eastern Europe* (pp. 283–320). Brookfield, VT: Ashgate.
Jelavich, B. (1983). *History of the Balkans*. Cambridge: Cambridge University Press.
Jelavich, B., & Jelavich, C. (Eds.). (1974). *The Balkans in transition. Essays on the development of Balkan life and politics since the eighteenth century*. Hamden, CT: Archon Books.
Jones, G., Hellman, J. S., & Kaufmann, D. (2001). *'Seize the state, seize the day' state capture, corruption, and influence in transition*. Transition Economies Working Papers. Washington, D.C., WA: World Bank.
Lampe, J. R., & Jackson, M. R. (1982). *Balkan economic history, 1550–1950: From imperial borderlands to developing nations*. Bloomington, IN: Indiana University Press.
Love, J. L. (1996). *Crafting the third world development: Theorizing underdevelopment in Rumania and Brazil*. Stanford, CA: Stanford University Press.
Mazover, M. (2000). *The Balkans. A short history*. New York, NY: The Modern Library.
Metzo, K. (1999). Reasserting peripheries in post-communist studies. *Special Issue of Anthropology of East Europe Review, 17*(2).
Minassian, G. (2002). The economic environment in Albania, Bulgaria, Macedonia and Greece. *Eastern European Economics*. Armonk, NY: M.E. Sharpe.
Ministerul Agriculturii si Alimentatiei (MAA). (1999). Programul National pentru Dezvoltare Agrara in Romania. Bucuresti: MAA.
Mitchell, B. R. (1998). *International historical statistics: Europe 1750–1993*. New York, NY: Stockton Press.
Mitrany, D. (1951). *Marx against the Peasant. A study in social dogmatism*. Chapel Hill, NC: University of North Carolina Press.
Pryor, F. L. (1992). *The red and the green. The rise and fall of collectivized agriculture in marxist regimes*. Princeton, NJ: Princeton University Press.
Recanatini, F., & Broadman, H. G. (2001). *Seeds of corruption: Do market institutions matter*? Transition Economies Working Papers. Washington, D.C., WA: World Bank.
Roberts, H. L. (1951). *Rumania: Political problems of an Agrarian state*. New Haven, CT: Yale University Press.
Rosenstein-Rodan, P. (1959). *How to Industrialize an Underdeveloped Area*. Cambridge, MA: Center for International Studies, Massachusetts Institute of Technology.
Roucek, J. S. (1939). *The politics of the Balkans*. New York, NY and London: McGraw-Hill.
Spulber, N. (1966). *The state and economic development in Eastern Europe*. Bloomington, IN: Indiana University Press.
Statistical Office of the European Communities, and Office for Official Publications of the European Communities. (2001). *Eurostat Yearbook*. Luxembourg: Office for Official Publications of the European Communities.

Sugar, P. F., & Lederer, I. J. (1994). *Nationalism in Eastern Europe*. Seattle,WA: University of Washington Press.

The Research Institute for the Quality of Life. (2000). *Report. A Journal Dedicated to Quality of Life and Social Policy*. Bucharest: Romanian Academy, The National Institute for Economic Research.

Tismaneanu, V. (1995). *Political culture and civil society in Russia and the new states of Eurasia*. Armonk, New York, NY: M.E. Sharpe.

Tismaneanu, V. (1998). *Fantasies of salvation: Democracy, nationalism, and myth in post-communist Europe*. Princeton, NJ: Princeton University PRESS.

Todaro, M. (1985). *Economic development in the third world*. New York, NY: Longman.

Verdery, K. (1995). *National ideology under socialism: Identity and cultural politics in Ceausescu's Romania*. Berkeley, CA: University of California Press.

Wädekin, K.-E. (1982). Agrarian policies in communist Europe. A critical introduction. In E. M. Jacobs (Ed.). (Vol. I). Totowa, NJ: Allanheld, Osmun & Co.

World Bank. (2001). *World development indicators 2001 (English)*. World Development Indicators. Washington, D.C., WA: World Bank.

Chapter 4
The Post-communist Period (1989–2000). Land Reform Between Property Rights Restoration and the Reorganization of Work and Production Relationships in Agriculture

Abstract This chapter explores the basic ideas and models underlying the agricultural reform policies in post-communist Romania, around the turn of the twenty-first century, during the period its policies were transitioning to be fully shaped by the European Union accession process. The chapter captures the dynamic before and during this moment. The analysis focuses on the legislative policy measures and tries to reconstruct from their structure and intended objectives, the underlying concepts and theories that guided the process of policymaking around this pivotal period. In parallel, this chapter argues that the efficiency consequences that were supposed to follow from the restoration of the private ownership of the land in agriculture were less impressive than initially expected.

Keywords Post-communism · European union pre-accession period · Land reform · Land restitution · Agricultural policy · Institutional reform

This chapter explores the basic ideas and models underlying the agricultural reform policies in post-communist Romania, around the turn of the twenty-first century, during the period its policies were transitioning to be fully shaped by the European Union accession process. During this period, the European integration process becomes increasingly a crucial determining factor for all domestic policies and a critical threshold is reached in becoming the main driver of the policy process. The chapter captures the dynamic before and during this moment. The analysis focuses on the legislative policy measures and tries to reconstruct, from their structure and intended objectives, the underlying concepts and theories that guided the process of policymaking around this pivotal period. In parallel, this chapter argues that the efficiency consequences that were supposed to follow from the restoration of the private ownership of the land in agriculture were less impressive than initially expected. Once the basic concepts and ideas were articulated and once a preliminary evaluation of the policy reform outcomes was made, the premises for evaluating the policy learning hypothesis would be created and a better perspective on the reform process in Romanian could be offered.

It should be noted that (the important political democratization process aside) two major socio-economic processes were set into motion as pillars of the post 1989 transition to the market economy and post-communist reform: the privatization of

A. Dabu and P. D. Aligica, *Economic Dualism and Agrarian Policies*,
SpringerBriefs in Economics, https://doi.org/10.1007/978-3-030-47836-0_4

the industrial sector, and the land reform in agriculture. Both processes radically changed the ownership structure of the Romanian society and the organization of the production relationships. Consequently, they had two important results: from an economic point of view, they changed the efficiency and growth capacity of those economies, while from a social perspective, they set into motion profound changes at the level of the existing social relations, especially at the level of the organization of the production relationships. Both the economic and the social aspects of the changes were directly determined by the new, predominantly private ownership structure that was introduced. In spite of the fact that the restoration of the private property of the means of production was a process of equal importance for the restructuring of both the agricultural and industrial sectors, given their structural differences, the introduction of private property rights took place in different ways in the two sectors and raised different types of problems for the policy makers and for society as a whole.

4.1 The Land Law 18/1991

After the radical political changes Romania went through at the end of 1989 (and except for the year 1990 when State officials were divided and still hesitant about the restoration of private land ownership rights), policymakers practically equated reform in agriculture with the restoration of the private ownership of land.

The law that set into motion the whole process was the *Land Law 18/1991* adopted by the Parliament in February 1991. The law was modified seven times between 1991 and 1997, most substantially by the Law 169/1997. The core aspects of the Land Law 18/1991 were as follows:

1. The law was based on the restitution principle up to a limit of 10 ha per family and it followed the land ownership structure of 1948. The minimum limit of land to be received was set at 0.5 ha. The maximum surface of land to be owned by a person was limited to 100 ha. If the pre-collectivization owners of land were no longer alive, heirs could claim ownership rights over the land.
2. Select social categories—active members of the former socialist production cooperatives who had not contributed land into these by the time of land nationalization, victims of the 1989 Revolution or their heirs, and people willing to settle in less populated rural areas—could get up to 10 but no less than 0.5 ha of land even if they had not contribute land to the former production cooperatives. In these cases, they could not sell their land for a 10-year period.
3. Only individuals holding Romanian citizenship could own land.
4. Land owned but not cultivated was subject to fines and the possible loss of the right of possession after two years of non-cultivation.
5. The liquidation procedure for the former production cooperatives was to be administered by a 'liquidation commission' to be established in a maximum of 15 days after the passing of the law in Parliament. The commission was

responsible for the lawful liquidation of the production cooperative and, once established, had to complete the liquidation procedure in a maximum of nine months.

6. The new landowners were presented with two options to organize production: they could either farm individually, or they could set up new associations by pooling together the newly distributed land. Fixed assets of the former, socialist production cooperatives as well as animal stock were to be distributed only to the newly established associations. Peasants deciding to farm individually (i.e. not to pool the newly distributed land in collective associations) were to receive only creditor rights over those assets proportional to (i) the land that had been initially nationalized and contributed into the former production cooperative and (ii) the volume of labor the former member of the cooperative had contributed over time.
7. State farms (*"intreprideri agricole de stat", abbreviated as "IAS"*) were to be converted into *commercial agricultural companies* according to the laws 15/1990 and 31/1990. Both laws were also regulating the privatization of the industrial and services sectors. In consequence, land nationalized over the communist period but held by state farms could not be restituted. Instead the former owners could get shares in the newly formed commercial agricultural companies.
8. No land taxes were to be collected until 1996. The period was later extended.
9. Changes in the uses of farmland belonging to legally incorporated associations were to be approved by the local and/or State authorities (i.e. Ministry of Agriculture and Food and Ministry of Water, Forests and Environment Protection). Individual farmers had to notify the Office of Land Registration and Organization within 30 days about any changes in the use of farmland.
10. The prevention and amelioration of soil degradation was to be largely financed and coordinated by the State, through both the Ministry of Agriculture and Food and the Ministry of Water, Forests and Environment Protection.

Two ideas guided the philosophy of the land law. First, restitution was regarded as the most legitimate way to compensate the rural population for the harms suffered during the harsh period of collectivization, regardless of any other efficiency considerations, or potential organizational difficulties implied by the process (Sarris & Gavrilescu, 1997: 193). Second, once land was restituted or distributed toward definite categories of owners, the associative form of the organization of production was to be favored over individual farming. Dismantling the former socialist production cooperatives was intended as a radical change in *the property rights* over land but less as a change in *the organizational aspects* of agricultural production. The law encouraged the new owners to continue to pool their land in production cooperatives, now called agricultural companies ("*societati agricole*"). This intention was obvious in the way in which fixed assets and livestock belonging to the former production cooperatives were to be redistributed. Fixed assets "that belonged to the abolished production cooperative, as well as the land on which they are placed, the vineyards, orchards and livestock became the property of the members of private associations, legally incorporated with juridical identity, if these will be set up. [. . .] Former members of the cooperatives, that do not become members of the new association will receive creditor rights, proportional to the share they are entitled from the patrimony of the production cooperative" (Article 29/1). Only in cases where no new production associations were being set up, were the fixed assets to be sold through public auctions toward individuals or other commercial entities with juridical personality (Article 29/3). The law thus framed, clearly favored the setting up of agricultural companies over private farming. Moreover, *continuity* was preferred to *the breaking-up* of the former production cooperatives and their reorganization in the form of either *new* farming associations or private farms.

Interestingly, in spite of the fact that the law did not ban the setting up of more than one new production association, no indication was given in respect to the way the fixed assets of the former production cooperative were to be divided among several potential associations if this were the case. Clearly, the expectation was that *only one* new association was to be set up, initially at least, and get the patrimony of the former production cooperative. This subtle difference was of major importance for the further functioning of the agricultural sector. Land restitution in the agricultural sector resembled very much the MEBO (Management-Employee Buy Out) privatization method used in the privatization of various industries or services sectors. Therefore, it borrowed many of its shortcomings. The main problem was that the ownership structure was changed but it did not bring about a radical change in the *organization* of work and production. The major problem generated by the Land Law 18/1991 was not the fact that associative farming was preferred to private, individual farming (although this may be a discussion in and of itself) but that various possible associative forms in agriculture were not realized in practice because the *continuation* of the former production cooperatives under a new juridical form was preferred.

There were several reasons why this way of distributing the fixed assets was favored. First, the distribution of fixed assets was technically much more complicated than the restitution/distribution of land. Second the village *nomenklatura*, made up by the former production cooperatives managers and technical personnel, favored the idea of agricultural associations. They were the first to benefit from the new system and to get information about its functioning. Most importantly they had good downward and upward market connections (i.e. the input and beneficiary industries), which the average person in the countryside lacked. Combined with the fact that many of the new landowners were no longer living in the countryside—about 40–45% of the new landowners were no longer living in the proximity of the localities in which they received property titles (NPADR, 1999: 14), and given the aged labor force in the countryside (the average age of the active labor force working in agriculture was over 50 years)—many landowners decided to pool land in the new production associations. Obviously, asymmetrical information and risk-averse behavior explain much of this decision as several authors noted (Brooks & Meurs, 1994; Mathijs & Swinnen, 1998), but as we tried to point out, the way the Land Law was framed and the interplay of various interest groups, such as the former village *nomenklatura*, played a central role in the process as well.

Irrespective of how significant the role of interest groups was in the shaping of the law, it is important to note that two leading ideas or principles have been behind the whole process. First, the restoration of private property rights in agriculture was seen by the overwhelming majority of politicians and technocrats as essential for the development of a market-oriented agriculture in Romania. That by the end of a decade of transition processes, Romania was still largely characterized by subsistence agriculture—a clear indication of the failure to reform the agrarian sector—bitterly proved, however, that by itself the restoration of private property was insufficient in generating agrarian markets and economic efficiency. Second, the law implicitly favored the large size farms, the presence of which was considered as one of the essential determinants of efficiency gains in agriculture. At the same time, the spirit of the law was such that it generated, paradoxically, an extreme land fragmentation and the formation of *new* associations was not encouraged. The most the peasants could get by forming new associations, was access to more labor and not to the capital of the former production cooperatives.

A 1991 World Bank-Romanian Government survey (Brooks & Meurs, 1994: 25) describes the effects of the law as follows: 62% of the households intended to pool their land and farm collectively, 35% expected to farm individually, while less than 25% opted for a mixed strategy (i.e. to farm part of the land individually and to pool another part in collective associations). The trend continued in 1992 too, when an estimate of 4050 formal and 11,500 informal associations had been established. However, in 1992 only about 43% of the arable land was farmed in both formal and informal associations, while individual households farmed 49% (the difference of 8% belonging to the State) (Bulgaru cited in Brooks & Meurs, 1994: 26). In addition, land fragmentation was high, a fact that could not come as a surprise given that the land law followed the 1948, pre-collectivization, ownership structure. In 1948, 91.1% of the households had holdings of less than 5 ha (Muresan & Muresan, 1998: 337). In 1992, 96% of the households owned plots of less than 10 ha, of which 63.6% owned less than 3 ha.

The number of both types of associations (i.e. with legal identity and informal) decreased over time in favor of individual farming. The phenomenon was more noticeable in the case of informal associations, which by 1999 represented less than half the number of those established in 1994. Moreover, peasants preferred the informal associations to the legally formalized ones. Over the entire period taken into consideration, the number of informal associations was constantly two to three times higher than the number of associations with formal legal identity (Table 4.1).

While the fragmentation of land could have been easily foreseen, the fact that almost half of the land was privately farmed in 1992 was rather surprising, especially in the context in which, as we tried to show, the land law favored associations over individual farming. Moreover, the share of land farmed in associations decreased by 10% between 1994 and 1999. Overall, by 1999 only about 20% of the agricultural land privately held was farmed in associations, both legal and informal (Table 1.1). This situation suggested that farming in association was associated with high transaction costs that did offset the benefits of pooling the land. These transaction costs seemed to be even higher in the case of formal associations (i.e. with legal identity).

Table 4.1 The evolution of the organization of the private farming sector 1993–1999

	1993	1994	1995	1996	1997	1998	1999
Arable land privately farmed (thousand hectares)	11,006	11,212	11,381	11,539	11,612	11,690	11,921
Production associations with legal identity							
1. Number	4265	3970	3973	3759	3912	3578	3573
2. Agric. land (thousand ha)	1910	1771	1733	1752	1714	1558	1416
3. Average size (ha)	448	446	436	466	438	435	396
Informal production associations							
1. Number	13,772	13,741	15,915	15,107	9489	7175	6264
2. Agric. land (thousand ha)	1763	1537	1596	1440	1000	950	869
3. Average size (ha)	128	112	100	95	105	132	139
Individual farms							
1. Number	3,419,736	3,578,234	3,597,383	3,625,758	3,973,329	3,946,121	4,119,611
2. Agric. land (thousand ha)	7333	7905	8052	8348	8897	9182	9377
3. Average size (ha)	2.1	2.2	2.4	2.3	2.24	2.33	2.28

Source National Program for Agriculture and Rural Development (1999, Annex 34); Buletin Informativ al Ministerului Agriculturii si Alimentatiei iulie (2000, p. 4)

Individual farms gained ground over associative farming for several reasons. First, land ownership by itself did not give way to a market-oriented agriculture in Romania. In the aforementioned survey, "nearly three-quarters of the households reported the land they claimed to be enough for their household" (Brooks & Meurs, 1994: 24). As the restoration of private land ownership was not accompanied by technological advances, rural credit and rural infrastructure development, the behavior of households was subsistence- rather than market-oriented.

Second, contrary to its own stipulations, the implementation of the law, especially the distribution of property titles proceeded very slowly and was still ongoing by the end of 1999 (Table 4.2). This law implementation failure slowed down the emergence

Table 4.2 Land property titles (p.t.) issued between 1991 and 1999

Year	Annual number of property titles issued	Share of the total number of p.t. issued yearly	Cumulative % of p.t. issued yearly
1991	25,963	0.60	0.60
1992	81,780	1.88	2.48
1993	592,564	13.68	16.16
1994	857,551	19.80	35.96
1995	843,085	19.46	55.42
1996	439,992	10.16	65,58
1997	188,174	4.34	69.92
1998	188,245	4.35	74.27
1999	125,934	2.90	77.17
Total	3,343,288	77.17	

Source National Program for Agriculture and Rural Development, Ministry of Agriculture and Food (1999: 13)

of the key institutional infrastructure of agriculture: an active land market, the emergence of land leasing and other associative arrangements as well as the development of the rural credit.

Third, until the end of 1997, state financial support continued to be primarily directed toward the remaining state agricultural sector. According to the National Program for Agriculture and Rural Development (NPARD) most of the state-subsidized rural credits had been received by this sector. Although the private sector ensured 80% of the agricultural production, only 20% of the subsidized credits went to the private sector, and then, most probably to the newly established formal associations (NPARD, 1999: 50). Thus, after four decades of socialized agriculture, with the passing of the Law 18/1991 and Law 36/1991 (to be discussed below), the organization of production was left to itself and pinned down by a singular reform pillar: the reorganization of property rights. There was no explicit state strategy as to how alternative production organization forms (i.e. individual farming or various associative farming arrangements) could be conceptualized, designed and made to coexist or compete successfully. At the micro-level, individual farming and subsistence production come to be perceived as the most, if not sole, feasible option—a situation that the Ministry of Agriculture and Food came to regard in the end as sub-optimal.

Fourth, at the end of the socialist era, the endowment with agricultural machinery, set aside its technological level, was very low. In 1991, only about 7% of the households owned any type of agricultural machinery, with "households themselves list[ing] access to machinery as their first reason for choosing to farm as part of an association" (World Bank-Romanian Government Survey 1991 in Brooks & Meurs, 1994: 28). The statistics issued over the period 1989–1999 by the Ministry of Food and Agriculture showed an increase in the number of agricultural machineries that belonged to the private sector. However, no information was provided regarding the share of machinery belonging to households farming individually *versus* in associations. It is more plausible that, relative to individual farms, associations remained more capital-intensive. Notably, while almost 10% of the active labor force switched from other sectors of the economy to agriculture between 1989 and the end of 1997, the share of land individually farmed increased by the same percentage by the end of 1998. With the collapse of various state industries. the unprecedented transfer of active labor force towards agriculture further amplified the labor-intensive character of the Romanian agriculture and deepened its subsistence orientation. Agriculture continued, thus, to be one of the most important employment options for a significant part of the country's labor force. By the turn of the century, 48% of the respondents to a nationally representative survey listed 'working in agriculture' as a possibility in case they would lose their present workplace "by tomorrow" (Barometrul de Opinie Publica, 2000: 63).

4.2 The Law Regarding the Agricultural Companies and Other Forms of Associations in Agriculture (Law 36/1991)

Adopted in May 1991, only a few months after the passing of the Land Law 18/1991, this law regulated the establishment and functioning of the new production associations, called "agricultural companies" ("*societati agricole*"). The main stipulations of the law were as follows:

1. The law introduced two types of associations: "simple" and with "legal identity". The simple, i.e. informal associations were to be formed by verbal or written agreement between parts. These associations did not have legal status. By contrast, the associations with legal identity, i.e. "agricultural companies" were to be listed in the Registry of Agricultural Companies.
2. A minimum of 10 members was required to form an agricultural company.
3. Land contributed to the associations continued to be the private property of the associated member. Fixed assets and livestock were considered in kind contribution to the social capital of the association.
4. The social capital of the company was divided in "social shares" of equal value. Each member was entitled to several social shares according to one's own contribution in land and/or in kind. To qualify for membership status, land contribution was enough.
5. The legal responsibility of a member toward the company was limited to the social shares one owned.
6. The organizational structure included: (a) The General Assembly formed by all of the company's members; (b) The Administrative Council with a minimum of 3 and a maximum of 13 members elected by the General Assembly from among the company's members; (c) The Directory Committee elected by the

Administrative Council. This organizational level is optional; (d) The Censors Commission elected by the General Assembly.

7. At least half plus one members of the Administrative Council were to be present when decisions are made. Decisions by the Administrative Council could be made only with two-thirds of the votes. At least two-thirds of the General Assembly's members had to be present to validate a decision. Important decisions, such as changes in the company's activity structure or the disbanding of the company could be taken only with two-thirds of the votes.

Many of the effects of the law have already been mentioned above. Initially, the law resulted in a high percentage of landowners willing to pool their land and form associations. However, given the lack of managerial skills in the countryside after years of planned agriculture and the relatively lower education level in the rural population, many peasants chose to farm either individually, or in informal associations. Associations with juridical personality required managerial skills that many of the peasants did not have. In this respect, the transaction costs implied by associations with legal identity seemed to be exceedingly high and the law proved too complicated to be easily understood or applied. In the absence of ample, well-organized training programs, its implementation remained in many cases accessible only to the rural *nomenklatura*, the managers of former production cooperatives, agronomists, and technicians. Consequently, among the new landowners that opted for associative farming, a majority become members of simple, informal associations.

As regarding the evolution of associative farming over the decade in question, it is worth noting that even if the decrease in the number of associations with juridical identity was not as drastic as in the case of informal associations, after 1993 the dismantling of associations was a constant phenomenon (Table 4.1). Also, taking into consideration that the average size of land farmed in associations with legal identity was in general four times greater than that farmed in informal associations, the decrease in the number of agricultural companies was of major importance for the new structuring of the organization of production in agriculture.

Regarding the efficiency of the associative farming sector, Brooks and Meurs's (1994) study showed that, by the end of 1991, the agricultural companies proved to be less efficient than individual farming, that they continued to hire more workers than necessary and that they continued the practice of the former production cooperatives of borrowing despite outstanding debts. Briefly, although these were new legal entities, many of the new agricultural companies continued the economic practices of the older production cooperatives. The fact was intensified by the relatively high number of associated members—an average of 193 members was found by a 1992 survey (Ianos cited in Brooks & Meurs, 1994: 25)—with limited individual power over the management of the company. This state resembled closely the situation encountered in industrial and service firms privatized by the MEBO method.

4.3 The Land Leasing Law 16/1994

The Land Leasing Law was adopted in April 1994, three years after the restitution of land had been established by the Land Law 18/1991. The law underwent significant modifications in 1998, when a new *Law 65/1998 for the modification and completion of the Land Leasing Law 16/1994* was adopted.

Land leasing was regarded as a supplementary way of consolidating land in larger farming units. However, land leasing is not only a matter of economic organization but also a matter of social and historical practice if not a social institution (Basu, 1984), the practical effects of the law were slow to form. The practice of land leasing, although old and still very popular by the turn of the nineteenth century, had gradually decreased between the two world wars. The successive land reforms that took place had conducted to the redistribution of land from large *latifundia* towards the peasantry. On the measure that land ownership become more egalitarian, the practice of farming under land leasing arrangements lost ground. By 1941, only "about 28% of land was held in lease or *metayage*, while less than 1% of the exploitations were entirely on rented land" (Roberts, 1951: 51). During the communist period land leasing had completely ceased and with this, the memory of the practice as a workable institutional arrangement was lost. Moreover, given the egalitarian principle that guided land restitution, a major structural condition for the emergence of land leasing arrangements, namely the existence of unequal land distribution, was not present in Romania. Yet, many of the current owners no longer lived in the areas in which they held land, and there was, thus, potential for land consolidation through leasing arrangements.

As in the case of the laws discussed above, the leasing law, at least in its 1994 form, had elements that prevented its large application. First and most important the leasing period stipulated by the law was of minimum 5 years (Article 7). The idea was probably that the leasing period be long enough to stimulate some minimal land improvements by the tenant. However, clearly defined property rights as well as law enforcement are essential conditions for the establishment of formal leasing arrangements. Unfortunately, by the end of 1994 only about 36% of the property titles had been distributed (Table 4.2) and it is reasonable to believe that fear of losing the ownership rights over the leased land might have made the law unattractive. The five years leasing period requirement was repealed in 1998 only.

Another important aspect concerned establishment of rent. The law mentioned that the rent could be paid in kind, in money or a combination of both. There was no clear reference to the various ways the leasing contracts may be concluded. The law proposed neither a pure fixed-rent tenancy system nor a pure share-tenancy system. Instead, the law mentioned that: "the rent to be paid in kind, will be established in a certain quantity of products, to vary between a minimum and a maximum production range" (Article 15). The same rule was to apply for rent paid in money, with the only difference that the amount to be received by the landlord reflected the monetary equivalent of the products at local markets prices (Article 16). Apparently, a sort of shared-tenancy system was encouraged despite the known Marshallian inefficiency[1] characterizing this leasing arrangement. The choice was probably motivated by risk-sharing considerations in case of bad crops and by the fact that "landlords" in Romania were not in a powerful position, i.e. land was abundant and extremely cheap. The landowners could hardly impose a fixed-tenancy system, even if it allowed for output maximization.

In any case, the formula of the law in respect to the rent calculus was confusing, the reference to minimum and maximum production levels being in practice unnecessary for the conclusion of shared-leasing contracts. This framing made room for either the underestimation of production by the tenant, or its overestimation by the landlord. The calculus of the rent based on a simple percentage of the total production would have avoided both situations. Four years later, the Law 65/1998 that amended the Land Leasing Law 16/1994 did not retain any indication relative to the calculus of rent. It only stated that the rent was to be established by mutual agreement and paid at the time and place indicated in the contract (Law 65/1998, Article 13).

One of the most important aspects of the Law 16/1994 was that it introduced the first reference to the privatization of the remaining state agricultural sector. The procedure was the following: individuals owning shares in *commercial agricultural companies* in which the State was a majority owner, were given the choice to become tenants ("*locator*") of the land over which they initially held shares. The leasing contract should have been signed for a period of minimum five years, by the end of which land property titles were to be issued. In other words, in order to get direct ownership rights, an individual's status had to transition from that of *shareholder* to *tenant* and after five years, to that of *direct owner.* The intention was probably to have a gradual transfer of property rights, one that would not disrupt too rapidly the prevalent status quo in the state agricultural sector. The established transfer period was however too long.

4.4 Law 54/1998 Concerning the Legal Transmission of Land

The Law 54/1998 established the legal basis for the creation and strengthening of the land market in Romania. Before its adoption in 1998, the legal circulation of land was regulated by a special chapter of the Land Law 18/1991. The law 54/1998 abrogated that chapter and brought multiple clarifications to the 1991 Land Law.

First and most important, the legal limit of land to be owned in Romania was increased from 100 ha per household, as had been established by the Land Law

[1] The English economist Alfred Marshall (1842–1924) considered shared tenancy to be an economically inefficient land tenancy institution. Marshall argued that under conditions of shared tenancy the total agricultural output tends to be sub-optimal. Marshall showed that given the nature of microeconomic decisions what is optimal from the tenant's point of view does not coincide with the societal level of optimal agricultural output. In general, under conditions of shared tenancy, the number of labor units invested by the tenant is smaller than what the "society" prefers.

18/1991, to 200 ha per household. Second, land ownership continued to be granted to Romanian citizens only. However, in comparison to the Land Law 18/1991, the new law was more liberal, in that it recognized land ownership rights to all the Romanian citizens, whether they had legal residence in Romania or not. Third, the law defined the two ways in which land could be legally transacted: (1) by buying and selling transactions and (2) by land holdings exchanges.

Co-owners, neighbors and tenants were given the right of first refusal. The law requested owners to formally notify the local authorities about the intention to sell land, while these had the obligation to make the offer public. Co-owners, neighbors and tenants could express their intention to buy the plots within 45 days since the offer had been made public. Although the right of first refusal represented a limitation of the landowner's property right, it was introduced with the intention to consolidate larger, compact land holdings. Again, the law was more liberal in spirit than the Land Law 18/1991. The right of first refusal was granted strictly to the above-mentioned categories. Unlike before, state entities had no right of first refusal. Moreover, the law allowed the landowners to refuse to sell their land to potential buyers with rights of first refusal in cases where a price agreement could not be reached.

Regarding the land holdings exchanges, the most important aspect clarified by the law was that State-owned agricultural land could not make the object of land holdings exchanges. Previously, State-owned land holdings could be exchanged against private holdings with the express approval of the Ministry of Food and Agriculture or the Ministry of Water, Forests and Environment Protection respectively. This former rule allowed for many discretionary and corrupt bureaucratic decisions.

Despite the adoption of a well-elaborated law regulating land transactions, the land market in Romania was still very poorly developed. Except for land in the vicinity of big cities or in tourist areas, agricultural land prices were extremely low. As a result, land consolidation through buying and selling remained very limited throughout the 1990s. Contrary to the opinion that de-collectivization and high land fragmentation would be conducive to the transactioning of land mainly through buying and selling (Trivelli, 1997), the land market in Romania remained poorly developed and inactive. As long as the agricultural production in Romania was not firmly driven by market demand and remained to a significant extent subsistence-oriented, it was very difficult to have an active land market in place. Relatedly, one of the most important conditions for the development of the land market was the existence of agricultural input prices (e.g. pesticides etc.) that were not offsetting the prices of the agricultural products. This condition was not met. What became slowly obvious was that by themselves, neither the existence of a well-elaborated law that regulated land transactions, nor the very de-collectivization process and the resulting land fragmentation, would result in a land market able to induce scale-efficiency.

4.5 Law 1/2000 for the Restoration of the Ownership Right Over Agricultural and Forestry Land According to the Land Law 18/1991 and the Law 169/1997

The political consensus that emerged ten years after the land restitution principle had been first affirmed by the Land Law 18/1991 was that land restitution was still incomplete and had to continue. The Law 1/2000 was passed in January 2000 with the aim to enhance the land restitution limit from 10 ha where it had been initially capped by the Land Law 18/1991 to a maximum of 50 ha of agricultural land per de-possessed person. Whereas all the prior legislation had focused on the restitution of land compulsory nationalized and held in *agricultural production cooperatives (CAPs)*, this new law focused on land that had been nationalized by the State and came to be farmed during the communist period in the so-called 'state agricultural enterprises' ("*intreprinderi agricole de stat*" abbreviated as *IAS*) and other state owned agricultural institutions such as agricultural research stations and institutes.

As has been already mentioned, based on the Land Law 18/1991, the former state farms (IAS) had been transformed into *commercial agricultural companies*, with the former landowners (or their heirs) owning 30% of the companies' capital in the form of shares. The remaining 70% of the IAS's capital continued as state property throughout the 1990s. Thus, if the Land Law 18/1991 led to the dismantling of the collective production farms (CAPs) while leaving the so-called state-owned sector mostly unaffected, this time the law allowed for the privatization of the former IASs *and* the restitution of land belonging to them.

In comparison to the very slow and ambiguous land restitution course enacted by the Land Leasing Law 16/1994 discussed above, the restitution process was this time radical and speedy. The law established a one-year period for the issuing of all the new property titles, including the still pending 20% property titles established in virtue of the Land Law 18/1991. In other words, it was expected that by January 2001 the historic process of land restitution and the distribution of land property titles would be finally concluded. The law mentioned that land had to be given back as much as possible on its pre-collectivization location. Only where this was no longer possible, were other locations to be considered. If current land availabilities were insufficient for all the lawful restitution demands, the former owners were to receive appropriate reparations in lieu of land.

An important albeit insufficiently elaborated aspect of the law, concerned the irrigation systems that had been built over half a century on land to be now restituted. The law required the owners of land on which such systems were in existence to make these accessible to all the owners in their proximity. In addition, the users were required to contribute proportionally to the maintenance of the irrigation system and were to be collectively responsible for possible damages, could the individual responsibility not be established. However, the law did not clarify the governance and property status of the irrigation system, i.e. state, private or common property. More precisely, the law eluded to specify if the owners of land holdings with pre-existent irrigation systems were to also become owners of these systems.

Given that irrigations represent a classical example of commons, their management may be difficult and conflictual. The fact that the law failed to define their property status and did not clarify how the *rules of usage* were to be established and enforced was a major shortcoming of the law. Again, and again, the legislators failed to anticipate the broader institutional fabric that needed to be simultaneously initiated to make the legislation stick. And the numbers spoke for themselves: if by the end of 1989 more than 3 million hectares of land were irrigated, in 2000 only less than 100 thousand were irrigated. In the year 2000 alone, losses due to severe drought were estimated to over 40% of production (Adevarul, 2000). Whether or not this was a classic case of public goods and free rider failure is a separate discussion not to be engaged at this point.

4.6 The Governmental Ordinance 198/1999

By this ordinance, in December 1999, the government decided to privatize the commercial agricultural companies that were still State owned. Over 600 such companies were targeted by the ordinance. By this measure, the privatization of the State agricultural sector was expected to come to an end. The ordinance was complemented by the Law 1/2000 discussed above, that established the way in which part of the land belonging to the companies should be restituted to the former owners. The privatization process was to be mainly coordinated by the Ministry of Agriculture and Food through a newly established institution—The Agency of the Public Domains ("*Agentia Domeniilor Publice*") and by the State Ownership Found.

Two distinct privatization methods were stipulated in the ordinance: (1) share purchases and (2) actives selling. The first method was preferred because it did not result in the dissolution of the company but only in the change of its ownership status. Only if a company could not be privatized through the first method, were the actives of the company to be sold to individuals or other formal associations and would the company virtually dissolve.

Although the privatization of the remaining State-owned companies in agriculture was supposed to proceed at an accelerated pace, the results of the Ordinance were rather disappointing. The change of the Government as a result of the 2000 elections slowed down the process. In fact, the new Government was less willing to privatize the former State-owned agricultural enterprises. The Government's program made no specific reference to the future status of these enterprises and provided only a crisis-management policy package emphasizing State support to the agricultural sector and further subsidization of a large range of agricultural activities (Sinteza Programului Năstase, Ziua, 2000).

4.7 Outlook of the Romanian Agriculture at the End of the 1990s, on the Threshold of Speeding up the EU Accession Process

At the end of the 1990s, as a result of the agricultural policies initiated in Romania, and especially of the weak performance of the industrial sector, a significant percent of the active labor force transferred to agriculture. In a comprehensive document analyzing the situation in agriculture at the end of the first transition decade, elaborated by the Romanian Ministry of Agriculture and Alimentation, it was acknowledged that " between 1989 and 1997, the increase of the share of agriculture in the employed active labor force by 9.3%,[2] and in the value added by 4.9%, has given the Romanian economic transition the character of an incipient *reagrarization*" (NPADR, 1999: 11, emphasis added). However, except for the remark that this process could have "unfavorable implications on the trend of social labor productivity" as a result of "the relative reduction of the share of investments in agriculture", the document had nothing else to say. It was unclear if what worried the Romanian policy makers was the absolute increase in the active labor force employed in agriculture or the process of de-capitalization that took place in agriculture and in the absence of which the stabilization of the new population in agriculture would have been somewhat less problematic.

To sum up, a major moment in how the relationship between agriculture and industry structured, occurred during the land reform that took place in Romania as well as in other Eastern European countries shortly after the radical political changes of 1989. Like the Czech and Slovak Republics, and Bulgaria and Hungary, the Romanian land reform after 1989 has been based on the principle of restitution. Given the pre-collectivization structure of the property an extreme fragmentation of the land followed. Thus, at the threshold of the EU accession process, about 44.5% of the agricultural land was owned by individual households with an average size of less than 2.5 ha[3] while another 10% had an average size of less than 5 ha. The document quoted above notes that this sort of agricultural farms "practice a subsistence agriculture, with the largest share of production being aimed for self-consumption" (NPADR, 1999: 60). This situation was clearly foreseeable given the fact that high fragmentation of land was a constant characteristic of the Romanian agriculture from 1864, when the first land reform was enacted, to 1945 when the last land reform (before the start of the collectivization process) was conducted.

Another significant aspect of the transition period was the constant increase of the gap between agricultural production and the production of the food industry. Despite

[2]To give a dimension of this phenomenon we should note that at the end of 1998 the share of the active labor force employed in agriculture, calculated on the basis of data available in the CESTAT Statistical Bulletin, no. 4/1998 represented 5.54% in the Czech Republic, 7.54% in Hungary and 19.08% in Poland. In Bulgaria the share of agriculture in total employment was of 22% in 1993 (Mathijs and Swinnen, 1998).

[3]In the European Union countries (EU-16) the average size of the agricultural land in individual farms is of 16.6 ha (NPADR, 1999, Annex 35).

the uncertainties brought about by the redistribution of land and the subsequent transformation of the structure of production in agriculture, agricultural output never fell below about 95% of its 1989 level.[4] However, during the period 1989–1998, production in the food industries went down by about 50%, except for 1990 when the production level was still at 80.7% of its 1989 level (NPADR, 1999, Annex 24).

Obviously, the subsistence character of the Romanian agriculture was not only a consequence of land reform with its extreme fragmentation, but equally, if not overwhelmingly, the result of a complete neglect of the relationship between agricultural production and its upward recipient industries. In fact, the behavior of the agricultural sector was rather puzzling to those considering the small farm size as an essential indicator for the low productivity level in agriculture.[5] Individual peasant households with holdings smaller than 5 ha made up about 55% of the Romanian enterprising agricultural units. In the context in which the capital endowment of agriculture, the use of fertilizers and pesticides, and the use of certified seeds decreased markedly, the performance of the agricultural sector was surprisingly good. Even more, the NPADR document mentioned that despite the output reduction, the agrarian sector was still the only economic sector to register constantly an increase in the value added (Annex 22:9). In conclusion, even if the organization of land and production in agriculture was still unsettled, it was far from being the main reason for the reverse process that Romania was facing by becoming increasingly agrarian. And yet, despite this evidence, the farm size and organizational aspects of agriculture continue to be the most debated subjects and the problem of agricultural development was still largely seen as a subject of its own, in isolation from the other sectors of the economy.[6]

Thus, this rather detailed overview of the agrarian reform policy legislation reveals that four basic ideas, models, or conceptual frameworks inspired the Romanian policy makers during this 1990–2000 period:

(a) Land restitution and private ownership of the land could by themselves solve to a large extent the problems of low labor productivity and output decrease, which took place during the period of planned agriculture.

---

[4]Exceptions are the years 1992, when agricultural output represented only 84,8% of the 1989 level and 1997, the only year between 1989 and 1998 in which agricultural production was higher than in 1989 and represented 102.7% of the 1989 level.

[5]As will be explained more fully in the next chapter, under the Marxist influence, a core idea of the Romanian agricultural development policy, especially in the post-World War II period, was the existence of a direct relationship between farm size and agricultural productivity. Large farms were seen as quintessential for the enhancement of productivity in agriculture. According to Marxist theory, small-size farms are associated with low labor productivity levels. Therefore, the organization of labor in large farms through collectivization was believed to lead to labor productivity enhancement in agriculture. However, the experience with collectivized agriculture in ECE did not support this assumption and several authors argued that the type of crops cultivated is an important intervening variable in the relationship between labor productivity and farm size (Pryor, 1992).

[6]Agricultural development cannot be regarded in isolation from the overall development of the economy, especially of its industrial sector. Therefore, the failure of agricultural development has to do not only to the low performance of agriculture as such, but at the same time with the incapacity to expand the industrial and service sectors of the economy to a level comparable to that characterizing advanced economies.

(b) Paradoxically, the large farm-size continued to be considered the ideal form of organization of production in agriculture, and the only one able to capture economies of scale in agriculture.
(c) Rural markets (e.g. of land, labor, and capital) were believed to emerge naturally as a result of the reintroduction of private property rights over land, a view remnant of the "organizational engineering" approach to agricultural development as opposed to an "institutional" understanding of its conditioning.
(d) A "pie" view of the economy, in the sense that agricultural development policies concern the agricultural sector in particular and can be designated in isolation from development policies concerning other sectors of the economy.

As it has already been mentioned, the results were not very reassuring. The question is in what measure the decision to develop policies influenced by those ideas was a sensible one, based on the previous experiences and an effort of learning from that experience. In order to answer that question, the study will move now to identify the ideas that inspired the reforms in the previous periods and will compare those ideas with the current ones, while at the same time considering the results of those past policies. The next chapter will analyze the 1864–1948 period, while Chap. 3 will be devoted to the communist period.

References

Adevarul. (2000, July 12). *Comunicat al Ministerului Agriculturii si Alimentatiei*. Bucuresti.
Basu, K. (1984). *The less developed economy. A critique of contemporary theory*. Basil: Blackwell Publisher.
Brooks, K., & Meurs, M. (1994). Romanian land reform: 1991–1993. *Comparative Economic Studies, 36*(2), 17–32.
Mathijs, E., & Swinnen, J. F. M. (1998). The economics of agricultural decollectivization in East Central Europe and the former Soviet Union. *Economic Development and Cultural Change, 45*, 1–26.
Metro Media Transilvania. (2000, May). *Barometrul de Opinie Publica*.
Ministerul Agriculturii si Alimentatiei (MAA). (1999). *Programul National pentru Dezvoltare Agrara in Romania*. Bucuresti: MAA.
Ministerul Agriculturii si Alimentatiei (MAA). (2000, Iulie). *Buletin Informativ al Ministerului Agriculturii si Alimentatiei*. Bucuresti: MAA.
Muresan, M., & Muresan, D. (1998). *Istoria Economiei*. Bucuresti: Editura Economica.
Pryor, F. L. (1992). *The red and the green. The rise and fall of collectivized agriculture in marxist regimes*. Princeton, NJ: Princeton University Press.
Roberts, H. L. (1951). *Rumania: Political problems of an agrarian state*. New Haven, CT: Yale University Press.
Sarris, A. H., & Gavrilescu, D. (1997). Restructuring of farms and agricultural systems in Romania. In J. F. M. Swinnen, A. Buckwell, & E. Mathijs (Eds.), *Agricultural privatisation, land reform and farm restructuring in Central and Eastern Europe* (pp. 189–228). Brookfield, VT: Ashgate.
Trivelli, C. (1997). Land markets and land prices in the Central and European free trade agreement countries. http://www.fao.org/WAICENT/FAOINFO/SUSTDEV/Ltdirect/Ltan0017htm.
Ziua. (2000, December 28). *Sinteza Programului Nastase*. Bucuresti.

Chapter 5
The Pre-communist Period (1864–1945). Agriculture Between the Creation of Market Institutions and the Planned Economy

Abstract This chapter takes a closer look at the main turning points in the evolution of the Romanian modern agriculture and the structural reform policies that shaped it before the communist takeover of the country in 1948. It begins with the second half of the nineteenth century, when the overall modernization of the country and its opening to the West European markets started to accelerate. It then moves to the dramatic changes brought about by its entering in the Soviet sphere of influence at the end of the Second World War. The chapter looks at the nature of specific policies in the context of Romania's efforts toward modernization, groups them under meaningful categories, and provides a concise analysis of their technicalities, structural aspects and overall consequences for the process of agricultural development.

Keywords Economic modernization · Land redistribution · Land leasing · Cooperation and the cooperative movement · Rural credit · Institutional reform · Peasant economy · Peasant emancipation

This chapter takes a closer look at the main turning points in the evolution of the Romanian modern agriculture and the structural reform policies that shaped it. It begins with the second half of the nineteenth century, when the overall modernization of the country and its opening for the West European markets started to accelerate. It then moves to the dramatic changes brought about by its entering in the Soviet sphere of influence at the end of the Second World War. It will be shown that between 1864, when the first land reform was enacted in the Romanian Principalities, and up to the beginning of the collectivization process in agriculture in 1948, the large land ownership, the *latifundia*, was gradually dismantled through successive land reforms that distributed land to the peasants, transforming them into *owners* of the plots of land on which they had worked for generations. This process took place under the pressure of several social, political, and economic factors that contributed to the gradual elimination of the pre-modern organization of production in agriculture, one in which the peasant was *de facto* bound to the land and lacked political representation. However, while it is certainly true that the *social* and *political* status of the peasant changed dramatically from 1864 to the period of the 1921

A. Dabu and P. D. Aligica, *Economic Dualism and Agrarian Policies*,
SpringerBriefs in Economics, https://doi.org/10.1007/978-3-030-47836-0_5

land reform (brought about by the First World War), the main failure of the successive land reforms undertaken during this period was due to the fact that they did not manage to create an efficient and intensive agriculture, and that peasants' standard of living remained generally low.

Once Romania entered the Soviet sphere of influence at the end of the Second World War this sinuous modernization process was completely halted. The economy became highly centralized, the century-long effort towards private property rights enforcement, and the establishment of a new and more egalitarian land ownership structure in agriculture were reversed and the socio-economic evolution of the country fractured in unforeseen ways. Following the Soviet model, land was collectivized, and production reorganized in large-scale cooperatives, that were expected to function on the model of industrial enterprises.

The present analysis will pay only scant attention to the political background of the agrarian reforms and policies undertaken in Romania in the period under consideration. The intention is rather to look at their nature in the context of Romania's efforts toward modernization, to group them under meaningful categories, and to provide a concise analysis of their technicalities, structural aspects, and overall consequences for the process of agricultural development.

5.1 The Evolution of Agricultural Organization from 1864 to 1917

By the turn of the nineteenth century agriculture represented the main sector of the economy and was dominated by large *latifundia* owned by the *boyars*—landowners, which also represented the upper political class. If from a juridical point of view peasants were 'free' (i.e. they could leave the latifundia on which they were born), in practice they could not become landowners and remained economically and socially bound to the boyars and their land.

The relationships between peasants and boyars were largely governed by social customs and informal rules. The most important among them was the unwritten rule requiring the landowners to give a piece of land in use to any newly married peasants living in the villages on their estate. By custom, landowners had the obligation to allocate up to two-thirds of their land to the peasants. The death of both husband and wife meant that the land went back to the landowner, only to be redistributed to other new, young families. The peasants had the obligation to work on the boyars' land an established number of days per year—a rule called "*claca*"—and to give the landowner part of the harvest. Importantly, by custom, peasants had free access to the commons i.e. grazing land and forests.

However, once the Romanian Principalities gradually escaped the Turkish rule and the Romanian landed class gained increasing control of the country's political structures, the relationship between boyars and peasants began to change in significant ways: it became much more formalized from a juridical point of view, and the olden customs that governed their relationships started to lose ground. In general, the boyars were now in a better position to introduce new *legal* rules that worked in their own favor. The evolution of agriculture in the nineteenth century was marked on the one hand by the gradual political independence from the Turkish Empire and on the other by the increasing access to and integration with the West European grain markets. At the same time, the economic condition of the peasants worsened (Mitrany, 1968). This paradoxical situation was mainly due to the peasantry's nearly complete lack of access to the political process. It was also due the fact that the bourgeois class was extremely limited and could not act as a check and balance for the power of the landed class, as had been the case in the Western part of the continent.

In 1856, by the Treaty of Paris the Romanian Principalities became autonomous. The Turkish Empire maintained a formal control over them until the 1877 War of Independence. Being placed under the protection of the Great Powers for all this period, The Romanian Principalities enjoyed extended autonomy in their political and economic life. The country was to be governed by native princes and by a liberal Constitution. In 1859 the two Romanian provinces of Moldova and Muntenia became united into one kingdom under the Prince Alexander Ioan Cuza. Prince Cuza, governed the country until 1866 when he was forced to abdicate and was replaced by the foreign but able King Carol I, brought on the Romanian throne by the Great Powers.[1] Transylvania was to remain part of the Austro-Hungarian Empire until the end of the First World War in 1918. The present analysis will focus only on policies and agrarian reforms undertaken in the provinces under formal Romanian rule, although this is obviously an oversimplification. Up to the unification of 1918, there were strong commercial relationships and an active circulation of ideas between the Romanian Principalities and Transylvania that put their mark on the agrarian policies adopted in the Romanian Principalities.

5.1.1 The Land Reform of 1864

The Reform of 1864, the first to distribute land to some categories of peasants, was introduced against the stubborn opposition of the landed class, through princely decree and only after Prince Cuza resorted to a coup d'etat on May 2nd. To do this, the Assembly—the legislative body of the country that repeatedly failed to pass an agrarian law in favor of the peasants and in line with the provisions of the 1856 Paris Treaty—had to be dissolved. Thus, this first land reform was primarily undertaken under external pressure, namely under the political pressure exercised by the Great Powers. It did not come about as a democratic decision of the Romanian political body or as a solution for the country's modernization generated from within.

An important characteristic of the reform, which was to become a constant feature of subsequent land reforms, was its *legalistic* approach. The peasants' rights to land were never justified on economic grounds or out of efficiency considerations. Even

[1] King Carol I reigned from 1866 to 1914.

the most enlightened and liberal minds of the time limited their arguments to the legal inconsistencies that would have followed from denying all *citizens* equal rights. The argument was that such a situation would badly hamper the *constitutional* basis of the new state. As Mitrany (1968) pointed out, what hastened the movement toward the emancipation of peasants was merely the impact of the humanitarian and egalitarian ideas brought about by the French Revolution and the adoption of *written* constitutions in all of Europe (and by necessity in Romania too). As he put it: "Nothing could have seemed to these men more abhorrent than the lack of personal freedom: their main ambition was to free the peasant from servitudes" (Mitrany, 1968: 50).

The goal was to put an end to the feudal relationships seen now through the lenses of the new political philosophy as unjust and had little if nothing to do with a vision on the country's future economic evolution. If in the West the emancipation of the peasants came at a time when the Industrial Revolution had been set into motion and a growing middle-class of industrialists and traders had emerged, in the East and in Romania in particular, these conditions were missing. Therefore, though animated by similar values, the emancipation of the peasants and the end of their customary servitudes were to have very different consequences for the dynamics of economic life in the two parts of the continent.

The main lines along which the reform was organized were as follows: (1) all labor servitudes were abolished, and (2) land was to be distributed to select categories of peasants, the *clacasi* (i.e. peasants holding in use a piece of land granted by the landlord and bound in exchange to various servitudes towards him). The poorest peasants were not entitled to land and received only one lot for the house and the surrounding garden, and (3) the amount of land to be received was differentiated according to the heads of cattle possessed by the household. The law established three categories of peasants, each getting a certain surface of land (see Table 5.1), (4) landlords were to receive compensations for the expropriated land. One-third of the compensation was to be paid by the State and two-thirds by the peasants themselves over a fifteen-year period, and (5) land could not be sold for a thirty-year period.

The size of the holdings was lowest in Muntenia were the ratio of peasants to land was higher. In the less populated regions, the average size of the holdings were

Table 5.1 Land distribution per historical regions and categories of peasants, according to the 1864 agrarian law

Categories of peasants	Land received per household (hectares)		
	Moldavia	Muntenia	Bessarabia (Cahul, Bolgrad and Ismail districts)
With four oxen	7.26	5.51	8.67
With two oxen	5.72	3.57	5.86
With one cow	3.04	2.05	3.05
Land for house and garden	–	–	–

Source Muresan and Muresan (1998: 107)

somewhat higher. However, most of the households belonged to the second and third categories respectively, with only about one fifth of them owning four oxen or more.

As a result of the 1864 Rural Law, 511 896 households received land in property, representing an area of 2,038,640.26. The average size of the plot was of 3.98 ha per family. From the country's total agricultural land 30% belonged now to the peasants, 60% to the landlords while the difference of 10% was state-owned (Muresan & Muresan, 1998: 107).

The structural aspects of the Romanian society and economy as compared to its Western counterparts, and the *implementation* of the reform as conducted by the landed interests, made of the 1864 land reform a practical failure. Not only did the economic aspects as expressed by the production levels and their qualitative structure worsen for a while, but the very social goals looking to end the peasants' servitudes in agriculture had been perverted. By the end of the reform, not only did the landlords manage to maintain the old servitudes of the peasants but they were also able to make them more severe than before.

Land was to be allotted from two sources: through the partial expropriation of landlords and from the State Domains. The State Domains originated mainly in the monastical estates that had been "secularized" only a year before, in 1863. About 25% of the country's agricultural land had become State property through the secularization law of 1863.

Before the reform, the landlord allotted land *by custom* to the newly married peasants and the allocations could have gone up to two-thirds of his estate. This rule had now been eliminated. Through abuse and misinterpretation of the law, the boyars managed to own more than half of the country's arable land, with no obligation whatsoever toward the newly married. Overall, as many peasants as possible were classified in the lower categories so that the landlords had to give up less land and could maintain more land under their ownership.

Similarly, the adoption of the law brought about the abolition of the old social custom of peasants' free access to the commons—forest and grazing lands. In exchange, peasants received small areas of forests and grazing land, which were soon to be transformed into arable land, as peasants were pressed by the payments of the annuities. Over time this situation resulted in a marked decrease of the livestock.

Another peculiarity of the law was that land allotted to the peasants did not in general coincide with the one they used to farm up to the enactment of the agrarian law. The allotted land was often of poorer quality. Under these circumstances, peasants found themselves increasingly unable to pay the annuities. Moreover, as the wheat markets were booming, the price of land grew several times, making the buying of land virtually inaccessible to the peasants. In order to pay the annuities, peasants were bound to *sell* their labor to the landowners under very unfavorable terms. This phenomenon came to be known as the "neoserfdom" period (Dobrogeanu-Gherea, 1910).

As Mitrany (1951, 1968) showed, this land reform, of major importance for Romania's later economic evolution, left the *organization of production* in agriculture unaltered. What had changed was the legal status of land ownership, which was now modeled entirely on Western standards. In respect to the technical aspects of production, and especially the endowment of agriculture with machinery, the situation remained basically unchanged, while the social character of the relationship between peasants and boyars worsened.

5.1.2 The Laws Concerning the Sale of Land from the State Domains

Up to the end of the nineteenth century successive laws concerning the sale of land from the State domains were enacted in 1866, 1868, 1876, 1881, 1884, 1886 and 1889. Generally, these laws benefited the landlords, as the conditions stipulated for the selling of land largely disregarded the peasants' economic possibilities. In particular, the size of the land plots to be sold and the payment conditions prevented the buying of land by the peasants.

As a result, up to 1881, all land put up for sale by the State was bought exclusively by the landowners, despite the needs and demand for land manifested by the peasants. Only in 1881 was a limited number of peasants able to buy land, and this because the selling conditions had been somewhat relaxed. Relative to their real needs, however, the land surfaces bought by the peasants were modest. According to the statistics of the time, 6687 peasants bought a total of 31,297 ha of land (Mitrany, 1968: 71), meaning that the average size of the newly acquired plots was generally under 5 ha.

As concerning the law for the selling of land from the State Domains enacted in 1884 and amended in 1886, it resulted in the selling of 680 State Domains out of which only 39 were acquired by peasants. Not surprisingly the years 1888 and 1889 were marked by peasant uprisings that eventually resulted in the adoption of some new, more favorable selling conditions in 1889. This time, plots to be sold could only be of 5, 10, and respectively 25 ha. Only plots of 10 and 25 ha were to be sold by public auctions and could be resold later. The smaller plots of 5 were to be sold on credit and on very easy conditions (i.e. no prepayment was necessary, the annuities were low, no individual could buy more than one plot of land, and that plot could not have been resold for a minimum period of thirty years.) As a result, 546,593 ha of land had been sold to 106,714 peasants of which 105,165 bought plots of 5 ha only. Again, the more favorable selling terms had not been motivated by economic considerations but undertaken under the threat of more serious social upheavals. The same had been the case in 1878, when after the War of Independence from the Turkish Empire, 48,342 newly married couples received 228,328 ha of land in Dobrogea, an under-populated region gained back from the Turkish Empire at the end of the war (Opritescu, 2000: 89). In this case, the reasons were also not economic, as land had been promised to the peasants in exchange for their military enrollment.

5.1.3 The Laws on Agricultural Contracts

As has already been mentioned, the agrarian law of 1864 had abolished the labor servitudes of the peasants toward the landlords. On the one side and at least in principle, peasants could now enter in free economic transactions and they could freely sell their labor. On the other side, with peasants now owning farming land, the boyars were anxious that paid labor will be in short supply. Hence, the first concern was to make sure they could ensure a high enough labor supply for the farming of their land, especially at the peak time of the harvest season. Moreover, the situation was aggravated by the fact that boyars did not possess the agricultural equipment necessary for the farming of land. By custom, this equipment was in the possession of the peasants.

The successive laws on "agricultural contracts" adopted in 1866, 1872, 1882, and 1893 were supposed to regulate the rural labor market. As in the case of the laws concerning the selling of land, these laws pushed the peasants under extremely disadvantageous conditions. At least until the adoption of the law of 1882, the agricultural contracts were conceived to block almost entirely the development of a functional labor market and to conserve as long as possible the former organization of the production relationships in agriculture (even if under a new juridical form attuned to the spirit of the new Constitution).

The preambles to the agricultural contracts laws of 1866 and 1872 stated openly that the "Rumanian agriculture had not reached the state when it might work with free labor" (Mitrany, 1968: 73). These laws allowed for the payment of rents or other monetary debts toward the boyars, to be commuted in labor obligations. As already mentioned, however, peasants had become increasingly indebted shortly after the agrarian law of 1864 and as the rural credit was virtually nonexistent, their labor obligations tended to become perpetual. Moreover the so-called agricultural agreements ("*invoieli agricole*") could be collective in nature and, in spite of the fact that *joint* responsibility was outlawed, in practice if a peasants could not perform his labor obligations, a member of his family or another co-signer of the agreement was asked to complete the obligations in his place. There was thus perpetual vacillation between the impetus of the new Constitution and the fall back on the old, custom-based governance type characteristic of the pre-1864 land law.

To make things worse, the law of 1872 introduced an amendment according to which military assistance for contract enforcement became lawful. In other words, the landlords could benefit from the direct intervention of the army, would the villagers run away or refuse to perform their labor obligations at the time contractually established. From a juridical point of view, this meant that labor contracts in agriculture were basically taken out of the sphere of the common law to which they normally belonged. By contrast, there was not a single law article ensuring the legal protection of the peasant in the face of potential contractual abuses by boyars.

The situation of the peasantry became so extreme that, when a new law on agricultural contracts was finally enacted ten years later, the legislators felt necessary to expressly stipulate that Fridays and Saturdays were to be reserved for the peasants' own needs (i.e. these were days on which peasants could not be asked to work on boyars' land). The same law abolished both the possibility of military contract enforcement and the joint responsibility stipulation. Moreover, only specific tasks were to be governed by contact, and these had to be clearly related to agricultural activities and could not exceed what a peasant and his family could typically perform in a definite time period. These contracts were to be renewed every year. Most importantly, labor remuneration was to be in cash only, and unlike before, the money could not be automatically retained by the boyar in virtue of a pre-existing debt of the peasant (Mitrany, 1968: 75; Opritescu, 2000: 88).

Up until the end of the nineteenth century, only one more law on agricultural contracts was to be enacted. From a historical perspective, the most important aspect of this law adopted in 1893 was contained in its final amendment, stipulating that labor contracts could be regulated by common law, would the parties to the contract so decide. It was the first recognition of the anomalous juridical situation of the peasant, one which had plagued him for almost thirty years.

This slow evolution of the regulations of agricultural contracts was possible only on the measure that agricultural machinery was slowly introduced in Romania and the population was growing. Both these trends relaxed the demand for compulsory labor. Even so, it took several years and the constant and energetic actions of Liberals such as Kogalniceanu and C.A. Rosetti (both of whom were interior ministers), before laws more favorable to the peasants could be enacted.

5.1.4 The Renting of Land

In the second half of the nineteenth century, the most remarkable change in the organization of production in agriculture was the emergence of the phenomenon of *absentee landlords* and with it the introduction of the renting of land on a large scale. After 1877 urbanization accelerated and the landed class started to prefer to the supervision of agricultural activities, the administrative and State functions. The renting of land became very popular. Only a handful of the boyars continued to live their lives in the old ways, most of them, especially those owning large estates of over 1000 ha, opting to lease their land (see Table 5.2). In comparison to the Western practices, the leasing of land in Romania took a peculiar form: it was seldom a direct economic relationship between landlord and peasant on the basis of which the latter would lease land against a certain established rent and the former would give land and agricultural machinery into use. Most frequently a *sublease* operation was also involved. Landlords preferred to lease all their land to one single tenant, that was often a foreigner and not a professional farmer and who in turn either subleased the land under disadvantageous conditions to several farmers, or hired labor, or used a combination of both these methods. Keeping up with tradition, the newly emerging social category of tenants, did not possess agricultural equipment, which continued to be provided by the peasants. In addition, as they usually rented the land for relatively

Table 5.2 The share of land properties leased according to their size at the beginning of the twentieth century

Land property area (hectares)	%
50–100	24.09
100–500	50.17
500–1000	58.23
1000–3000	58.33
3000–5000	73.36
Over 5000	72.43

Source Muresan and Muresan (1998: 134)

short periods of time, neither were they interested to invest in such equipment. Put otherwise, this new form of production organization did not stimulate technological improvements and agricultural machinery and cultivation practices remained stalled at the level of the rudimentary techniques the peasants could afford. The effect was the continuation of an extensive type of agriculture and the maintenance of an exceedingly large labor force in agriculture.

As in the case of the agricultural contracts analyzed above, cash payments of the rent were as much as possible discouraged in favor of their equivalent in labor. In practice, the combination of agricultural and leasing contracts delayed the development of a *monetary* economy in the countryside and by this of the habit of economic calculus typical for a modern society.

In 1907, four decades after the land reform of 1864 had been enacted and had put into motion a very sinuous development process of the rural economy (enormously complicated by various ill-conceived or ill-applied agrarian laws) one of the most violent and unfortunate peasants uprising exploded in both the two main historical regions that made up Romania at the time (Moldavia and Muntenia). The uprising was mainly directed against absentee landlords and their tenants and was stopped only by the extremely brutal intervention of the army: an estimated 10,000 peasants were shot. However, the uprising represented a very important turning point for the treatment of the agrarian question in Romania and for the change of the country's political climate.

The need for the improvement of the peasantry's standard of living as well as the numerous shortcomings of the former agrarian legislation came to be openly recognized in the Parliament by both the Conservative and the Liberal parties (Mitrany, 1968). The same year, a new law on agricultural contracts was adopted, one that substantially improved the 1893 law and limited drastically the privileges of the landlords, giving firm protection to the peasants against landlords' potential abuses. Child work was expressly outlawed. Also, the same law established the creation of village commons on land supplied by the State domains as well as on land sold by the landowners to villages (as administrative entities) at market value. As concerning the leasing of land, if before there was no legal limit in respect to the surface that could be leased by a person and in some notorious cases such surfaces reached as much as 237,000 ha, now this surface was limited by an antitrust law to 4000 ha. Also, in

1908 the so-called Rural Office ("*Casa Rurala*") was founded, a 50% State-owned institution with the purpose to help the transfer of land from large landowners toward the peasants. The office could buy land from the large landowners and re-sell it under advantageous conditions to the peasants, or it could mediate the selling and buying operations between landlords and peasants. The Office was also charged to inform the peasants about modern cultivation techniques and to encourage their use.

These were only some of the positive policy measures adopted by the Parliament shortly after the big peasant uprising in 1907. Even if many of them were not implemented in practice or had only partial effects, these measures certainly indicated an increased awareness and preoccupation of the political class and the State in respect to the social and economic problems of the peasantry.

To sum up, in the period from 1864 to the First World War, the extensive character of the Romanian agriculture deepened. Both the size of the total agricultural land and the country's population almost doubled (Table 5.3). Under the increasing demand for grains on the international markets, the cultivation structure changed in favor of wheat and maize that occupied the largest surfaces with 37.5% and respectively 40.8% of the grain cultivated areas. At the same time, the surfaces occupied by grazing land and forests decreased markedly, a phenomenon that caused in turn a decline of the livestock.

Another aspect of the Romanian agriculture in the period under consideration was the extreme overall sensitivity of the Romanian economy to the evolution of the corn prices on the international market. On average, grain production—especially wheat—was not lower in Romania than in other important grain exporting countries such as the U.S. and Argentina, but it was obtained with more labor intensiveness and at the expense of more advanced cultivation techniques. In 1905 about 75% of the country's population was making its life from agricultural activities (Muresan & Muresan, 1998: 128). Agriculture was, however, characterized by *underemployment*. At the beginning of the twentieth century the average number of working days in agriculture per person were estimated at 91 days a year.

Despite visible efforts to distribute land to the mass of peasants, the property structure remained very uneven. In 1905 large land properties of over 100 ha made up only 0.6 of the land proprietors in Romania but occupied as much as 48.7% of the country's total agricultural land. By contrast, the share of peasant holdings with an average size of less than 2 ha was over 47% (Table 5.4).

5.2 The Evolution of Agricultural Organization from 1917 to 1945

The most important event that called for a new major land reform, one that had been already urged by the Liberal Party after its coming into power at the end of 1913, was the breakout of the First World War in 1914. The increased recognition by important political leaders of the necessity to improve the economic situation of the peasantry,

Table 5.3 Agricultural land and population in Romania in the period 1860–1915

Years average	Agricultural land (hectares)							Year of the census	Population
	Total	Arable land		Grazing land		Orchards and vineyards			
	1000 ha	1000 ha	%	1000 ha	%	1000 ha	%		
1862–1866	12,334	3335	27.1	3668	29.7	147	1.2	1860	3,917,541
1896–1900	13,018	5845	44.9	2046	15.7	224	1.7	1899	5,956,690
1911–1915	13,327	6135	46.0	2053	15.4	185	1.4	1912	7,160,682

Source Axenciuc (1996: 47–48); Roberts (1951: 355)

Table 5.4 The structure of peasants' holdings according to the land area at the beginning of the twentieth century

Land area category (hectares)	%	Cumulative %
Landless households	23.9	23.9
0–2	23.2	47.1
2–5	36.0	83.1
5–10	14.0	97.1
10–50	2.9	100

Source Muresan and Muresan (1998: 133)

the need to ensure its participation to the war effort, and the tremendous effect of the 1917 Russian Revolution on the peasantry's *etat d'esprit* in all the neighboring Central and East European countries and in Romania in particular, determined King Ferdinand[2] to directly address the peasants. In a public address, he promised land to the peasants by the end of the war, would they vigorously support the country's war effort:

"Sons of peasants, who, with your own hands, have defended the soil on which you were born, on which your lives have been passed, I, your King, tell you that besides the great recompense of victory that will assure for every one of you the nation's gratitude, you have earned the right of being masters, in a larger measure, of the soil upon which you fought.

Land will be given you. I, your King, am the first to set the example; and you will also take a larger part in public affairs" (King Ferdinand quoted in Roberts, 1951: 23). The effect was tremendous and the army enrollment an devotion to the war effort unparalled.

5.2.1 The Agrarian Reform Laws of 1921

In June 1917, with more than half of the Romanian Kingdom's territory under German occupation and the government evacuated to Iassy in the still free territories, the Parliament agreed to modify the Constitution and adopted the principle of large estates *expropriation for "reasons of national utility*". Land expropriation began shortly after the war in 1918–1919 by decree and was completed by the passing of the Agrarian Reform Laws of 1921. The process lasted officially until 1926 although by 1930 land titles were still being distributed to the peasants. A total of 6 million hectares had been expropriated and distributed to the peasants in lots of no less than 5 ha. Land property was this time limited by law to 100 ha in the hilly and mountainous areas and to 150 ha in the plains. Only in exceptional cases, where the landlord had made substantive investment in agricultural machines and used the most advanced farming techniques, were farms allowed to consist of a maximum of 500 ha, but such cases were rare (Table 5.5). Only about 10% of the country's

[2]King Ferdinand reigned from 1914 to 1927.

Table 5.5 Farm size structure in Romania according to the 1930 rural census

Farm size (hectares)	%
0–5	74.9
5–20	22.6
20–50	1.7
50–200	0.6
Over 200	0.2

Source Muresan and Muresan (1998: 192)

agricultural land was now held in farms of over 100 ha as compared to over 40% before the reform. Put otherwise, through the land laws adopted by the end of the First World War, the large *latifundia* had finally come to an end. Small and medium holdings now occupied most of the agricultural land and this represented the most important change of the organization of production in agriculture.

The change was radical from both a social and a political point of view. On the one hand it modified markedly the production relationships in agriculture and on the other it contributed to the change of the country's political spectrum. The Conservative Party—representing the interests of the landed class—was simply wiped out from the political scene and in December 1918 the Peasant Party emerged. At the same time, the principle of universal ballot was introduced in the Constitution and peasants were finally getting the right to vote. Yet, as important as these changes were, they had not been driven by clear economic objectives and programmatic policies regarding agriculture's future evolution. The older organizational structure of agriculture dominated by large farms was not replaced because it was believed to be inefficient. As in prior instances, change was facilitated by demographic, political, and contextual historic circumstances.

After the 1921 Agrarian Reform Laws, with the peasant household as its main organizing principle, the problems of the rural sector may be summarized as follows: (1) land fragmentation, (2) overpopulation in the rural areas and under-occupation of the rural labor force, (3) decreasing prices of agricultural products both internally and on the foreign markets, (4) weak development of the institutions of the rural credit, and (5) poor endowment of agriculture with needed agricultural equipment and therefore low labor productivity. These problems were to be addressed through an uneven mixture of state interventions directed toward the support of the agrarian sector.

During the 1920s, an impressive number of institutions aimed at promoting rural development were put into place. Thus, in 1924, Agricultural Chambers were formed in each *judet* (county), in 1925 the Union of Agricultural Chambers was formed in Bucharest and in 1926 and 1927 respectively, the National Zootechnical Institute and the Romanian Institute for Agronomic Research were also brought into being. Underfunded and often with inadequate organizational structures (especially in the case of the Agricultural Chambers), these institutions designed to be centers for the dissemination of information with regard to modern agricultural techniques and production modes, achieved little of their generous objectives and remained generally ineffective or inaccessible to the peasants. Finally, while still dodged by policy makers in the 1920s, the most acute and in the end, the defining problem of agriculture the 1930s was the lack of sound rural credit institutions.

By the end of the 1920s, the credit-related problems intensified considerably, and an increasing number of peasants become unable to pay back their debts. The break-up of the world economic crisis of 1929–1933 only aggravated this context. The situation was particularly critical in its implications. On one side, debt payment incapacity would have normally triggered the loss of land and agricultural property by large numbers of peasants with very limited work alternatives outside the agricultural sector. On the other side, the banking sector itself was badly shaken, with large banks that could not recover their rural credits facing bankruptcy.

Between 1931 and 1934, several legal solutions were tried for the rural debt crisis. The 'technical' solution was the so-called *conversion of agricultural debts* but the practical transposition of this principle into concrete legal measures was controversial and hence, continuously recalibrated. As a result, between 1931 and 1934 five consecutive laws allowing for debts' conversion were adopted in order to redefine the relationship between debtors and creditors. Each of these laws either completely reversed or at least substantively modified the previous ones.

The law that was finally retained and implemented was the *Law for the Liquidation of Agricultural and Urban Debts* adopted in April 1934. The law established that debts should be paid back in a maximum 17 years, by bi-annual payments at 3% interest rates. Half of the total amount of the debt was waived, irrespective of the size of the landholding. The law also stipulated that 60–70% of the debt could have been further waved would the debt be paid off in five and respectively two years. According to the Ministry of Justice' statistics, over 2.47 million peasants (i.e. 71.4%), most of them with landholdings of less than 10 ha, asked to be considered under this law (Muresan & Muresan, 1998: 235). The numbers are indicative for the amplitude of the agricultural debts' crisis. Moreover, as several scholars noted, from the outset, most of these debts had been contracted not so much for productive reasons as for the covering of basic, subsistence needs and hence, did not translate in a significant increase of the rural sector's production capacity or overall productivity (Roberts, 1951; Muresan & Muresan, 1998; Opritescu, 2000).

5.3 The Great Depression of 1929–1933 and Its Impact on Agriculture

The economic crisis of 1929–1933 affected agriculture in major ways. Internally, the prices of agricultural products fell markedly. By the end of the crisis (1934) they were less than half their pre-1929 level. By comparison, the prices of industrial goods had deteriorated at a lesser extent and the prices of industrial goods required

Table 5.6 The evolution of price indices of agricultural and industrial products and of industrial products required by agriculture for selected years

Year	Price indices of agricultural products	Price indices of industrial products	Price indices of industrial products required by agriculture
1929	**100**	**100**	**100**
1931	50.8	72.0	86.6
1934	**44.1**	**63.4**	**82.6**
1935	48.4	75.2	90.2
1936	54.0	–	95.4
1938	**67.1**	–	**99.2**

Source Muresan and Muresan (1998: 291) and Roberts (1951: 177)

by agricultural activities had fallen even less, a situation that indicates the massive deterioration of the purchasing power in the agricultural sector and the amplitude of the "price scissors" (Table 5.6).

The prices of agricultural products fell sharply also on the foreign markets, a situation with tremendous effects for all the agrarian states of the region. Although from 1920 to 1939 Romania's export structure evolved significantly, with cereals gradually losing ground in favor of oil and other industrial products, the share of agricultural products remained nevertheless high over the entire period (Table 5.7). Consequently, the Romanian economy continued to be affected by the mercurial evolution of the international prices of agricultural products and grains in particular. According to Roberts (1951) during the 1929–1933 economic crisis "the average price per metric ton of Rumanian exports fell in 1934 by 62% of its 1922–1930 average, whereas the price of imports fell by only 33% in 1936" (177). Obviously, the deterioration of the exchange rate between domestic and foreign goods sharply reduced the capacity of international trade to generate economic growth.

From 1930 to 1939 the combined share of grains and oil products in the country's total exports never fell below 72.2%. The Great Depression not only resulted in

Table 5.7 The weight of Romania's main export products in the total exports for selected years

Year	Grains and derivates (%)	Oil products (%)
1920	**67.2**	**19.1**
1925	25.4	19.8
1930	**36.2**	**36.6**
1931	41.4	30.8
1934	22.2[a]	52.8
1935	24.5	51.7
1939	**31.9**	**41.9**

Source Muresan and Muresan (1998: 228, 296)
Note [a]Lowest level for the period 1920–1939

the stabilization of the international prices of agricultural products at much lower levels than before its break-out, but also gave rise to the adoption of protectionist agricultural policies in Europe's industrialized countries.

Between 1928 and 1931 Germany, France, and Italy had introduced high tariffs for the imports of various agricultural products. In counterpart, between 1930 and 1933, the Balkan countries, reunited in the so-called "agrarian block", tried to negotiate more favorable conditions for the export of their agricultural products, but their efforts were unsuccessful. The failure of international negotiations pressed the Balkan countries to resort to similar protectionist and price-supporting measures for their own agricultural products.

In Romania this situation inaugurated a period of constant state intervention in favor of the agricultural sector. Import controls were first introduced in 1932, and the state constantly encouraged exports through subsidies and the elimination of export duties on agricultural products. In 1934 the Office for the Export of Cereals was created and placed under the direct governmental control. Moreover, to prevent the collapse of prices, the state, through its newly created State Cereal Commission, bought the market surplus of grains for several consecutive years. And, after 1935, minimum state-guaranteed prices for agricultural products were introduced aiming to ensure stable revenues for the peasants (Mitrany, 1951; Muresan & Muresan, 1998).

These measures somewhat alleviated the situation of the rural sector but reached only marginally the mass of the poor peasants caught in a subsistence form of agricultural production. First, the bulk of the measures benefited the middle and especially large producers that were connected to the grain export markets, while having little effect on the small peasant holdings (Roberts, 1951). Export bounties targeted the production of wheat only, while the small producers were predominantly cultivating maize. Second, despite the existence of a wide political consensus on the need to gradually reduce the area under grain cultivation and reorient Romania's agricultural production toward the raising of livestock and the cultivation of better valued crops on the international markets (e.g. industrial plants, soy, sugar beet, and fruits), the perverse effect of the price-supporting policies was the maintenance and even the slight increase in the cultivation of cereals and wheat in particular (Roberts 1951; Muresan & Muresan, 1998). For instance, between 1930 and 1934, 84.4% of the arable land was under grain cultivation. This area decreased to only 83.3% in the 1935–1939 period. At the same time, between 193 and 1934 wheat represented on average 28.1% of the total area under grain cultivation and maize 43%. As a result of the aforementioned price-supporting policies, these numbers only increased. From 1935 to 1939, the area under wheat cultivation increased to 32.1% and the area under maize cultivation to 44.7% (Axenciuc, 1992: 51–53, 519–520). These numbers illustrate the weak capacity of successive governments to put into practice the desiderata proposed by several studies and internalized by the political parties themselves, as well as the reactive, non-strategic character of the measures undertaken by the state after the Great Depression.

If the practice of state intervention in the form of price supporting measures, favorable export tariffs, and export bounties for agricultural products was constantly reinforced during the 1930s, it should be mentioned that other types of agricultural policies, more *institutional* in character, were also tried even if only with limited impact. First, several laws aimed to enforce *rural cooperation* and *land consolidation* were adopted. Second, after the agricultural debt crisis of the early 1930s, *rural credit* was more systematically approached and reorganized.

It should be noted that the origins of the cooperative institutions and the institutions of rural credit in Romania went back to the nineteenth century. The cooperative and rural credit institutions created during the third and fourth decade of the twentieth century (to be discussed below) were built on these earlier foundations and represented a natural counterpart to the 1921 land reform. These institutional measures tried to address the problem of extreme land fragmentation that had spiked up after the 1921 Land Law, as well as to address the problem of peasants' endemic poverty. What was new, however, in the post WWI era was the increasing state influence over both the cooperative movement and the institutions of rural credit. During the 1920s, both sets of institutions had become more and more engulfed by restrictive state regulation, while during the 1930s and especially as a result of the interventionist climate that emerged with the Great Depression, their early logic was reversed or perverted. The spontaneous and grass roots character of the cooperatives movement lost much of its vigor and they became rather a reflex of state regulation that boosted their emergence and kept them alive thereafter.

5.4 Attempts for Land Consolidation and Enforcement of the Rural Cooperation Movement

The Law for the establishment of agricultural associations was passed by the Parliament in July 1931. The law aimed to encourage peasants to pull land in associations, a measure that was obviously trying to solve the problem of increasing land fragmentation brought about by the Land reforms of 1921 and which was aggravated by the further splitting of plots through family inheritance. The law allowed for preferential credits toward such associations, if they would reunite separate plots in an economic whole and if they would follow an economic plan previously approved by the Ministry of Agriculture. Whether because its requirements were too complex to follow, or the peasants lacked sufficient information, or the timing of the law was unfortunate—the beginning of the Great Depression and the break-out of the agricultural debts crisis—this law had very little practical impact. However, its adoption reveals legislators' awareness with respect to the problem of land fragmentation and subsistence agriculture. In a similar vein, but without greater success, in March 1937 a law banning the subdivision of land in plots smaller than 2 ha was adopted. Its enforcement proved however exceedingly difficult for the local authorities.

During the dictatorship of King Carol II (1938–1940), and for the first time after the landmark 1921 land reforms, the legislators' preference for medium and large-scale farming was openly reasserted. In 1938 a new Constitution was adopted, and further land expropriation and land redistribution were expressly prohibited.

King Carol II's regime openly asserted the importance of medium and large farms and its intention to form indivisible estates of roughly 10 ha. However, aside from a law adopted in December 1938 by which the state could buy land to be then resold under strict conditions to Romanian subjects in plots no smaller than 15 ha, little was said about the technical steps by which the objective of land consolidation could be reached. The selling conditions imposed by the law regarded the interdiction to further subdivide the land through selling or by transferring it to more than one heir. The law had little impact, if any, on the large number of small land proprietors unwilling to sell their plots to the state and unable to acquire larger estates advertised by the law. Kings Carol II's dictatorial regime came to an end in 1940, before the talk and plans in respect to agriculture—most notably his intention to diversify the structure of cultivation and increase total agricultural output by systematic, yearly investments in agricultural machinery—were put into action.

During the Second World War period (corresponding in Romania to two political dictatorial regimes) the agrarian question and the problem of extreme land fragmentation become secondary to that of mobilizing for the war effort. Nevertheless, in June 1942, a new law for the organization of agricultural associations was adopted. It was very similar in content with the aforementioned law of 193. The law encouraged peasants to form associations that were authorized to buy agricultural machines, seeds, fertilizers and so on and to sell the common production. As in 1931, the law provided for preferential credits under strict credit conditions. Again, such associations were to be placed under the strict administrative control of the Ministry of Agriculture and could not operate as authentically independent economic entities. The bureaucratic character of the law, the numerous restrictions it imposed, as well as the fact that it had been adopted during war time, made the law rather ineffective. By 1944 only an estimated 200 associations had come into being as a result of the law.

5.5 The Institutions of Rural Credit

For the period under consideration, the institutions of rural credit in Romania could be divided into two categories: (a) those originating in the cooperative movement, the so called rural credit cooperatives that later developed into popular banks, and (b) the private banks that directed their credit with predilection to agriculture. Notably, the banks belonging to these two categories came under the control and influence of the State either soon after being formed or were created from the very beginning with important State contributions to their capital (Mitrany, 1930).

As already mentioned, the first institutions of rural credit in Romania took the form of credit cooperatives that transformed later into popular banks. They established in Romania as early as 1891 and 1892 respectively and even earlier in the Romanian provinces still belonging to the Austro-Hungarian Empire, and that served as a model. By the break of the First World War the number of rural credit cooperatives had increased to over 700 and represented genuine grass roots organizations built "on the initiative and with the means of the villagers" (Mitrany, 1930: 378).

The 1903 law "Concerning Rural Popular Banks and their Central Office", the first to directly regulate the organization of rural credit in Romania, aimed to link these popular banks in a network of rural credit institutions. In practice though, the main effect of the law was the placement of rural banks under direct state control, through the newly created Central Office.

The State was to provide the popular banks with funds through the Central Office under strict administrative conditions stipulated in the law. The Central Office begun gradually to operate as a sort of central bank for the popular banks. The system that resulted was hierarchical in structure with the Central Office subordinated to the Central Bank and the popular banks under the subordination of the Central Office. By the end of 1927 an astounding number of 4773 popular banks were subordinated to the Central Office. Their coordination became even more hierarchical when federations of popular banks formed and interposed themselves between the Central Office and the popular banks.

This organizational structure had wide implications: state intervention in the administration of the rural credits grew steadily and bureaucracy hampered credit allocation. Interest rates charged by the popular banks, although generally three times smaller than in the private banking sector, were still artificially increased by the many intermediate levels interposed between the National Central Bank, that provided a substantial part of the funds to the Central Office, and the individual borrower. State influence grew not only as a result of the fact that most of these funds were now provided by the state but also because the personnel of the Central Office was nominated in large measure by the State.

This situation continued until 1929 when a new Law for the organization of Cooperation was passed. This law replaced the Central Office of the Popular Banks by a new institution of rural credit designed to enjoy large autonomy—The Central Cooperative Bank—with credit functions towards the entire cooperative movement in Romania. The voting power of the State in the managerial board was being limited to one third of the total votes even though half of the bank's capital was still government provided. In terms of granted loans, the overall performance of the new bank was however extremely poor. Its administrative organization took a very long time as it had to take over the actives and passives of the former 'Central Office' while at the same time establishing its own territorial structures. Its credit operations were therefore overly cautious, and the amount of credit granted to the rural sector exceedingly low. The break-out of the Great Depression only worsened this tendency.

Rural cooperation was not limited to the credit cooperatives. The cooperative associations were in fact very diverse. A variety of forms including consumer cooperative societies, cooperative societies for production, cooperatives of production and consumption, landholding and land-purchasing cooperatives coexisted at the same time. They were organized on the model of the rural credit cooperatives in regional federations coordinated by a Central Office.

In addition, other types of cooperative organizations replicated the same organizational model. On the model of the popular banks, production and consumers' cooperatives were reunited under the Central of the Cooperative Societies for Production and Distribution, established in 1919. As in the case of the Central Office of Popular banks, the personnel of this Central Office was nominated by state authorities, a fact that again deepened the lack of genuine political and economic autonomy of the cooperative movement in Romania.

In respect to the institutions of the rural credit, it should be mentioned that over the 1920s and more firmly over the 1930s, rural credit although disproportionately small relative to the real needs of agriculture or the capital directed toward industry, had nevertheless increased considerably. Another notable trend was the continuous growth of state intervention in the allocation and administration of rural credit.

5.6 The 1945 Land Reform

The last redistribution of land in Romania, before the start of the collectivization process, was paradoxically conducted by the first Communist regime—the Groza government that came into power in 1945. This last land reform allowing for further land redistribution to the peasants was introduced by law-decree on March 22, 1945 and was one of the first measures undertaken by the new Groza government. It was largely justified not by the Communists' credo in small proprietors in the countryside but as a tactical step undertaken supposed to ensure if not the loyalty of the large peasant population, at least its lack of opposition to the new regime. In fact, the reform went against the Marxist theory that held as a dogma a clear-cut, direct relationship between large property size and efficiency. As Roberts bluntly characterized the situation: "[…] it was not a Rumanian reform but had its sources in the Soviet Union, and […] its immediate aims were *political not economic*" (297, emphasis added).

The reform addressed specifically the poorest farmers as land was to be redistributed only to those having farms of less than 5 ha. Land in excess of 50 ha was *confiscated* (i.e. the expropriation was without compensation), irrespective of whether the owners directly cultivated the land or not. Relative to the 1921 land reform, the maximum farm size permitted by law was now cut down in half. As in 1921, exceptions were made in the case of well-off farms that could constitute model farms under the direction of the Ministry of Agriculture. These farms could maintain up to 150 ha, a limit much lower than the maximum 500 ha allowed for model farms by the Agrarian Reform Laws of 1921. Beside the general criteria that all properties in excess of 50 ha were to be expropriated, land belonging to absent landlords, land in excess of 10 ha not worked by the owner himself in the last seven consecutive years, and that of ambiguously defined categories such as land of 'war criminals', of German citizens or Rumanian citizens of German ethnic origin many of which were declared in bulk as Nazis collaborators was to be entirely confiscated. In fact, many abuses were made and large numbers of German ethnics suffered expropriation on the basis of their ethnic origin and a significant number of them were deported to Siberia.

The total land expropriated amounted to roughly 1.47 million hectares of which about 1.1 million were redistributed to landless peasants and to peasants holding less than 5 ha. The rest formed what was called the state reserve and was to be used for the establishment of the first state farms built on the Soviet model (the so called *gospodarii agricole de stat—GAS*) and the first state 'stations for agriculture machinery and tractors' (*statiuni de masini si tractoare—SMT*) (Muresan & Muresan, 1998: 338; Turnock, 1986: 180). A total of over 900,000 peasants benefited from land redistribution and received plots averaging 1.3 ha (Roberts, 1951: 296). Moreover, property confiscation extended to the agricultural machinery and livestock existent on the expropriated land and was proportional to the surface of land to be given up. The majority of the machinery—for instance 3135 tractors, and 2533 ploughs that were confiscated (Muresan & Muresan, 1998: 337)—were distributed the newly established state SMTs, only a minor share reaching the poor categories of peasants the law was supposedly targeting.

Overall, as expected, the proportion of farms of 1–5 ha in size increased (Table 5.8). The agrarian census of 1948 found that they represented 54.7% of the total number of agricultural enterprising units while the proportion of large holdings of over 20 ha had further decreased to only 0.7% of the agricultural enterprising units in Romania (Galopentia & Onica, 1948: 11). As in the case of past land reforms, the law denied the owners' right to sell, division, lease or mortgage the land received.

From an economic standpoint, the results were disappointing. Peasants' need for land could not be satisfied. Land holdings of less than 3 ha—considered by Romanian economists of the time too small to ensure the subsistence level for a family of four—were still representing 78.4% of the agricultural exploitations in Romania. Moreover, the timing of the reform and the way it was conducted by the Communist regime invited too many irregularities, arbitrariness and spontaneous take-overs of land. The immediate effect was a sharp decrease in production. In the long run, the 1945 reform did not address the issue of low labor productivity in agriculture, the over-fragmentation of land, and the problem of agriculture's overpopulation. These,

Table 5.8 Structure of land ownership by size, 1948

Size of property (hectares)	Number	Percentage
Less than 0.5	901,016	16.4
0.5–1	1,100,852	20.0
1–2	1,473,785	26.8
2–3	838,286	15.2
3–5	697,318	12.7
5–10	363,678	6.6
10–20	88,335	1.6
20–50	22,698	0.4
Over 50	15,170	0.3
Total	5,501,138	100.0

Source Galopentia and Onica (1948) in Roberts (1951: 297)

however, were not problems that the reformers intended to solve. As Mitrany (1951) remarked, for the very similar course of events that had taken place in 1921 during Russia's collectivization "the peasant had got practically all the land, but each had only a little" and "the peasant revolution had been only accepted because that was inevitable, and also because it was a convenient radical means of destroying the bourgeoisie economically. But Marxism in general and the Bolsheviks in particular had no ready agrarian program to fit the peasants revolution" (65–66). It was only three years later that the drive toward collectivization started in Romania. That drive was to fundamentally change the organization of production in agriculture and this in ways in which the peasants, the alleged beneficiaries of these policies neither anticipated, wished for or supported.

References

Axenciuc, V. (1992). *Evolutia Economica a Romaniei. Cercetari Statistico-Istorice 1859–1947.* Industria (Vol. I). Bucuresti: Editura Academiei Române.

Axenciuc, V. (1996). Evolutia Economica a Romaniei. Cercetari Statistico-Istorice 1859–19470. *Agricultura* (Vol. II). Bucuresti: Editura Academiei Române.

Galopentia, A., & Onica, P. (1948). Recensamantul Agricol din Republica Populara Romana, 25 ianuarie 1948. Bucuresti.

Mitrany, D. (1930). *The land and the peasant in Rumania*. New Haven, CT: Yale University Press.

Mitrany, D. (1951). *Marx against the peasant. A study in social dogmatism.* Chapel Hill, NC: University of North Carolina Press.

Mitrany, D. (1968). *The land and the peasant in Rumania*. New York, NY: Greenwood Press.

Muresan, M., & Muresan, D. (1998). *Istoria Economiei*. Bucuresti: Editura Economica.

Opritescu, M. (2000). *Istoria Economiei si Administratiei Publice in Romania*. Bucuresti: Editura ASE.

Roberts, H. L. (1951). *Rumania: Political problems of an agrarian state*. New Haven, CT: Yale University Press.

Turnock, D. (1986). *The Romanian economy in the twentieth century*. London: Croom Helm.

Chapter 6
The Communist Period (1945–1989). From Small Peasant Holdings to Large-Scale State and Collective Farms

Abstract This chapter focuses on the communist period, a time of radical and dramatic changes in Romania's agriculture and economy. The chapter outlines the radical changes that took place in the realm of agrarian policy in Romania during the Communist period, as compared to the pre-1948 private property-based agriculture. It also highlights the intellectual origins in the design of agrarian policies during this period as well as the constraints imposed by the totalitarian political system on the diffusion of alternative ideas about agricultural development.

Keywords Land nationalization · Collectivization · Industrialization · Economic development · Agroindustrial complexes · Dual economy · Marxism · Theory of economic development · Comecon · New economic mechanism (NEM)

This chapter focuses on the communist period, a time of radical and dramatic changes in Romania's agriculture and economy. The objective will be twofold: to outline the main concepts and theories underlying the communist agrarian reform experiments, and to investigate the policies implemented and their overall outcomes. As usually, the underlying theme of this approach will be the notion of policy learning from experience and policy analysis.

Probably the best starting point for a discussion of the socialist ideas and theories about the agrarian sector, and more specifically, about reform in the agricultural sector, is the classical debate that ensued initially in Russia (during the second half of the nineteenth century) between Marxists and Populists and that diffused later on in the East European space. At the core of the Marxist—Populist debate was a search for the understanding of the role of agriculture in development. Another major focus of the debate was on understanding the prospect of agrarian countries such as Russia and other East and Central European nations to follow Western patterns of development, with a view to the policy solutions amenable to the typical problems of that region. What is significant in the context of the present analysis is the relevance of the Marxist theoretical corpus of ideas and of the Populist (*narodniki*) reaction to them for our understanding of the ongoing problems of development. In fact, many of the theoretical problems that have been raised during this debate constantly resurfaced in the discussions of agricultural reform in Eastern Europe and in Romania.

A. Dabu and P. D. Aligica, *Economic Dualism and Agrarian Policies*,
SpringerBriefs in Economics, https://doi.org/10.1007/978-3-030-47836-0_6

Marxian theory of agricultural development had at its core the general "law of capital concentration" and thus, favored the idea of large-scale agriculture. Its corresponding agrarian strategy consisted in land nationalization and forced collectivization. The Populist movement (known in Romania as "*poporanism*") challenged the Marxist doctrine of agricultural development and especially opposed the idea of collectivization. The populists advanced a model of society that was completely centered on the peasant and on the forms of social organization typical to peasant societies.

A leading exponent of this line of thought summarized the idea as follows: "our economic evolution, as the whole structure of the State, will necessarily have to retain its specific peasant character. Hence, economic progress must tend above all to organize the nation's economic life on peasant foundations [...]" (Stere, quoted in Mitrany, 1951, p. 39). In later writings Stere advocated the need for "technical progress in agriculture" and pointed out the limited capacity of the peasant household to acquire modern equipment. In a publication from 1932 he commented: "All these requirements [the introduction of complex and costly machinery] cannot be realized by the isolated peasant households, they presuppose capitals, technical management, cultivated surfaces that by far exceed the resources of individual peasant households" (Stere, quoted in Murgescu, 1990: 191). Populists thought that the solution to the modernization of agriculture could reside in the development of *rural cooperation*, which was regarded as an indispensable condition for the improvement of the peasant's situation. In Romania, the idea of rural cooperation translated at the political level and become the core of the Peasant Party's doctrine (Murgescu, 1990: 262–271).

Although they were more favorable to the idea of industrial development, Marxists could neither overlook nor overcome the agrarian problem in their theoretical scheme of thought. Their approach failed to explain *how* the East could reproduce the Western pattern of development. More precisely, Marxists theory did not provide an explanatory mechanism of *how* to create a large vigorous industrial sector able to absorb on a voluntary basis large parts of the rural population. Moreover, as the Marxist goal was to build up a communist society through social revolution and the socialization of the means of production, the accent on the role of industry in development was more instrumental than substantial (Mitrany, 1951). The theory emphasized that industrial workers would serve the revolutionary goals much better than the peasants with their conservative mentality, and this was one of the main reasons why, as opposed to the populists, Marxists favored industrial over agricultural development. However, Marxists were convinced that the institution of private property had to be eliminated. In short, the Marxists wanted to see the western pattern of development unfolding in the East but without the western institutions (i.e. private property and markets).

The debate is thought-provoking, as it makes evident that development was believed to be not institution-related, but rather the result of adequate organizational forms of production. As Mitrany (1951) persuasively demonstrated, Marxist solutions to development were in sharp contradiction with the peasants' aspirations for land ownership, as well as with the intent of the first land reforms conducted in East and Central European countries starting with the second half of the nineteenth century.

The first wave of land reforms had put an end to the pre-modern agrarian relationships governing the Eastern and Central part of the continent transforming, for the first time, large numbers of peasants into landowners. As a consequence, at the end of the nineteenth century and during the first decades of the twentieth century, obsession with land nationalization, prevented Marxist socialists from gaining any substantial support among the peasant population (and this was the case in the Western countries as well). In practice, Marxists revolutionaries had to accept the preservation of private property in agriculture as a temporary solution, and even to initiate successive land reforms (i.e. redistribution of land from larger landlords towards large numbers of peasants), out of pure political opportunism (Mitrany, 1951; Roberts, 1954).

But, in fact, neither Marxists nor Populists were able to envision and implement coherent development paths for their countries. Although Marxists had a better sense of the role of industry in development and the trends in the global economy, they dismissed the importance of market institutions, especially the centrality of private property rights in development, and insisted upon the importance of industry out of purely ideological reasons: it was helping them reach the communist society. On the other hand, while the Populists were generally supportive of private property and private land ownership, they were reluctant to recognize the need for industrial development and overemphasized the possibility of an agrarian-based development path.

The sketch of the Marxist-Populist debate outlined here was intended to show the ideational origins of practices of agricultural development that were to be implemented only much later, at the end of WWII, when communist regimes took the power in Central and Eastern Europe. The debate corresponds to what Pryor (1992) calls the classical phase of the Marxist theory of agricultural development. Following the periodization proposed by Pryor (1992), the next section outlines the main turning points in the evolution of Marxist theory and practice of agricultural development and its reverberations in the Romanian context.

6.1 Outline of the Marxist Theory and Practice of Agricultural Development and Collectivization

According to Pryor (1992) the evolution of the Marxist theory of agricultural development can be divided into three distinct phases: the classical phase, the implementation phase, and the reassessment phase.

(I) *The classical phase* took place before the Bolshevik Revolution in Russia and was defined by efforts to conceptualize the long-run aspects of agricultural development. Though lacking in complexity, the corpus of ideas developed during this early period, greatly influenced the move toward collectivization in later stages. During this phase, a long-lasting debate emerged regarding the influence of farm size on economic efficiency in agriculture. Marx depicted large farms as being more productive than small farms because they allowed for economies of scale as a result of greater division of labor, more extensive mechanization, and easier access to agricultural technology. In this view, large farms were the equivalent of factories in the countryside and the organization of their production process could follow similar principles. As Mitrany (1951) puts it: "The core of Marx economic analysis, as of his theory, was an elemental belief in the superiority, and hence the necessity, of large scale production. This was clearly true in industry and could not but be true also in other fields of production. No part of Marx's economic theory was more uncritically accepted than this" (10).

Marx and Engels contended that the general evolution of agriculture would follow inexorable trends that conformed to general laws of historical evolution. Pryor (1992) identified five major theses concerning agricultural development in the writings of Marx and Engels:

1. The average land area of farms would become larger.
2. The farm sector would become increasingly differentiated, with the land being held by ever fewer people (concentration and centralization of capital).
3. The smallholder could not compete against large farms and would lose his land ("become annihilated"),
4. The small farmers would be transformed in proletarians.
5. The form of payments to the landlord would change from a system of labor rents to sharecropping and then, to fixed monetary rents.

Moreover, Marx's underlying sociological conception of the peasantry emphasized its reactionary conservatism, anachronism in the context of the industrial revolution, and its non-economic behavior (i.e. non-capitalistic, non-market, self-sufficiency orientated behavior). The *Communist Manifesto* for instance speaks about the "idiocy of rural life" and it is worth noting that this idea that the behavior of the peasant is fundamentally non-economic persisted in the economic literature until late in the twentieth century (Schultz, 1964, 1993).

(II) *The implementation phase* was subdivided by Pryor into a "canonical phase" (comprising the writings of Marx, Engels, Kautsky, Lenin), and the phase of the "later Marxist writers", or the Marxoid phase (including the writings on agricultural development of Stalin, Mao, and Cabral). Pryor argues that the ideological debates that took place in Russia and several Eastern European countries around Marx's theses and their implementation influenced the development strategies of many Third World countries.

(a) The canonical writers. On similar lines with David Mitrany, Pryor points out the political implications and practical difficulties posed by the vagueness of Marx and Engels' writings for what he calls "the canonical writers"—often notable members of various European social-democratic parties. Particularly in the eastern part of the continent socialists had to face the very practical questions of how and when the collectivization of agriculture should proceed. As Marxist theory offered little guidance in this respect, many of the canonical writers developed independent views as to how theory and practice could be reconciled.

> At the turn of the century some of the leading social-democrats, so for instance Eduard David in Germany and Otto Bauer in Austria, argued against the need for agriculture's collectivization and claimed that the peasant smallholdings proved their economic superiority, and that large scale organization is not as desirable in agriculture as it is in the industry. In Russia, Lenin too changed his position in respect to agriculture several times from the extreme view of the necessity of total land nationalization to a position similar to that held at times by Kautsky—to help peasants understand the benefits of collectivization through education, a process that Lenin feared could take an unforeseeable long time.

In Romania, the socialist Constantin Dobrogeanu-Gherea could also be considered among Pryor's canonical writers. His best-known book *The Neoserfdom*, published in 1910 provided an astute account of the social and economic contradictions brought about by the adoption of Western legal institutions ("the superstructure") in a context in which feudal relations of production ("the base") still characterized the vast majority of the population. According to Gherea, the mix of Western legal institutions with feudal socio-economic structures resulted in a new "monstrous mode of production", in which a superficial appearance of Westernization masked the vast continuation of feudal practices and relations of production. But Gherea's main aim was to analyze the prospects of Marxism in the context of the backward, agricultural countries of the East. In Gherea's view an economically independent peasantry was a precondition for the development of capitalist relations of productions in agriculture—a necessary precedent of the Communist mode of production—in these countries. However, he saw the empowerment of the small farmer only as a temporary solution and remained a strong supporter of industrialization. Announcing what was to become a theme of the post Second World War center-periphery theories, he noted: "A country eminently agricultural is a country eminently poor and socially and economically backward" (Gherea, quoted in Mitrany, 1951: 28).

Karl Kautsky, one of Marx's most notable disciples, argued in a book published in 1902 that the expropriation of small farmers would ultimately not be necessary, claiming that collectivization could occur on a voluntary basis, once the peasants realized the benefits of cooperative farms. However, at times he doubted that peasants would ever arrive at such organizational arrangements if not forced to do so (Pryor, 1992: 43). Kautsky also developed the argument that *service* cooperatives might be enough to ensure economies of scale in a small holdings-based agriculture (Pryor, 1992: 44), a rather undesirable possibility given the Marxists' hope to see the peasants transformed into proletarians. Some twenty years later, in a book published in 1923 the Russian agricultural economist A. V. Chayanov provided empirical arguments for the idea that the optimal farm size was relative to the *type* of farming activities. His findings also favored the creation of service cooperatives to capture economies of scale by the peasant households. Chayanov's work was extremely influential, although as Murgescu (1990) notes, "it did not match I.V. Stalin's thinking on the cooperativization of agriculture" (252, note 123) and did not, therefore, shape agricultural policies during the Communist period. However, as the same historian notes, in Romania, Chayanov marked profoundly the thinking of the economist Virgil Madgearu, a leader of the Peasant Party who held various ministerial functions between 1928 and 1933. Madgearu had already theorized the peasant household as a distinct form of economic organization, the superiority of which he claimed, derived from the elimination of salaried paid work as an economic category. The work by Chayanov, deepened his conviction that the peasant household needs to be treated as a distinct national-economic entity and that a combination of economic and sociological analysis is required for the proper understanding of its way of operation (Murgescu, 1990: 252–262).

(b) The Marxoid phase. Pryor makes the interesting comment that due to the pressure to come up with institutional solutions tailored to the internal context of their respective countries, the writers he included in this phase, "often isolate[d] one key factor of agricultural production on which to peg the major arguments [in favor of collectivization]: for Stalin it was land, and the most important institutional change was to combine small farms into much larger units; for Mao it was labor, and the most important policy step was to combine the labor efforts of previously isolated farmers; and for a disparate group of theorists (including Nikolai Bukharin, some members of the Left Opposition, and, a generation latter, Edward Kardelj in Yugoslavia) it was capital, and the most important institutional change was to create a capital intensive agriculture before collectivization could be successful" (Pryor, 1996, pp. 41–42). For the agricultural policies followed in Romania shortly after the coming of the Communists into power, Stalin's conception on collectivization had undoubtedly the most profound influence.

(III) *The selective reassessment phase* refers to the period that began in the 1980s in several communist regimes around the world and in which some of the basic economic arguments for collectivization began to be questioned. At the core of the debate was the question of whether the policy of extracting surpluses from agriculture in order to finance industry (i.e. to set the terms of trade against agriculture in order to finance the development of industry) was suitable. It should be noted however that some authors rejected the very idea that this policy ever took effect in practice.

In a comprehensive study of the Communist agriculture in Eastern Europe and the former Soviet Union, Johnson (1993) argued that the collectivization of agriculture did not contribute to the industrialization of the Soviet Union during the 1930s although he conceded that we may speak of exploitation in the rural sector (an estimated 5 million people died of famine in 1932–1933 alone and 2 other million *kulaks* were deported to Siberia and other remote areas of the former Soviet Union). Johnson brought evidence in favor of the idea that Stalin's agrarian policies resulted in the *transfer* of resources from the rural to the urban sector, including the industrial sector, but that this transfer did not constitute a base for capital formation in the industrial sector. Also, according to the same author, this conclusion could be generalized for all the Central and Eastern European countries because they narrowly followed the Stalinist model of agricultural collectivization.

Moreover Johnson argued that in the 1960s, as collectivization came to an end across the region, a new era also begun: as a rule, *the subsidization of agriculture* become inevitable and this policy worked uninterruptedly up to the fall of the communist regimes in 1989. An important piece of evidence for this switch in policy and in the treatment of agriculture is the increase in the share of investments made in agriculture. Despite the fact that agriculture's share of total national gross productive investment was not uniform among the ECE countries and the Soviet Union (in the Soviet Union this share was continuously increased over the time, reaching almost 30% in the late 1970s, while in countries such as Bulgaria and Romania this share decreased continuously to something less than 20%) in all the countries it was still superior to the contribution of agriculture to the national net material product. Moreover, Johnson shows, the real wages in agriculture were constantly much higher than the relative labor productivity in agriculture. However, the data provided for the relative wage in agriculture look exceedingly high and the conclusion that "agriculture is probably more capital intensive than the rest of the economy in these countries" (Johnson, 1993, p. 16) remains very questionable.

The analytical problem of the relationship between agriculture and industry in development aside, it is worth noting that during the selective reassessment phase of the 1980s the communist policy-makers came to realize that the organizational means to reform State agriculture had been exhausted and that the contribution of the private sector to the total agricultural output could no longer be underestimated.

6.2 Outline of the Evolution of Agriculture in Romania During the Communist Period

At the beginning of the 1950s when the collectivization process began in earnest, more than 70% of the country's active labor force worked in agriculture. According to estimations done by FAO (Food and Agriculture Organization) in 1960 this proportion had decreased to 64.5% and reached 49% in 1978. Post-transition, a study conducted by the Romanian Commission for Statistics at the end of 1998 found that 38.1% of the active labor force was employed in agriculture (hunting, forestry and fishing included) while the rural population as a share of total population was still as high as 45%. These bare data give us a good firsthand image on the socio-economic structure of Romania. Except for Albania, post WWII no other former communist European country had a larger share of its active population steadily employed in agriculture. As has been previously shown, this proportion diminished due to a rapid pace of industrialization. The protracted process of collectivization in agriculture was practically completed in 1962 only but in contrast with other countries the substitution of capital (machinery) for labor was much lower in the Romanian agriculture.

In consequence, despite the elimination of private land ownership that collectivization brought about, a large part of the population continued to be employed in agriculture. For comparison, in neighboring Bulgaria, a country that entered the communist era with a similar low level of industrialization, the collectivization process had been accompanied by a larger rate of labor to capital substitution and in consequence, the country's urbanization process was more rapid and the capitalization of agriculture more noticeable (Swinnen, 1997). If in 1978 the active population employed in agriculture represented 49% of the total active population in Romania, it represented 35.7% in Bulgaria.

Romania's industrialization policy imposed very high costs on the rural population. The effort required from the rural sector in order to supply the industrial sector with cheap food was tremendous and necessitated its strict control until the beginning of the 1960s. The economic burden was even more intense up to the end of the 1950s, as Romania had to pay war damages to the Soviet Union and the confiscation of the entire crop of the farmers—the so called 'obligatory quotas'—by the State was a common practice. At the same time, investments in the industrial sector were boosted by the indirect taxation of the agricultural output: the prices of agricultural products were set by the state at artificially low levels, while the prices of the industrial products were allowed to be much higher. In other words, the terms of trade were set against agriculture.

This was a general policy followed by many communist countries but with different degrees of intensity. In the case of Romania, given the initial low level of industrialization, this brutal development strategy played a very important role. As Wädekin (1988) put it: "Good natural endowment for agriculture and more than half a hectare of tilled land per head of population, combined with ample resources of agricultural labor, seemed to favor an economic strategy of extracting capital (food at low producer prices) and cheap manpower from agriculture for the benefit of the industry. Available capital inputs per hectare and per worker were and remained lower than in other East European countries with collectivized agriculture (except Albania)" (324).

However, at the end of the 1960s it had become clear that this policy could no longer continue without serious consequences for the entire economy. In all the East and Central European socialist countries, reforms directed toward the betterment of the situation of the rural sectors emerged.

Using the share of agriculture in the total economically active population as a classificatory criteria, Wädekin distinguished four groups of countries inside the European Eastern bloc: (a) with less than 10%: East Germany and Czechoslovakia, (b) 10–30%: Hungary, Bulgaria, Soviet Union, (c) 30–45%: Romania, (d) more than 45%: Albania. Apparently, Poland was not included in this classification because of its unique land ownership situation (as a result of a dramatic social upheaval in 1956, about 80% of the land remained in private ownership during the communist period). Wädekin's suggestion was that "[…] the countries of 'reformed orthodox' agrarian policy emerge as those with less than 30% agricultural employment. […] The utopian and radical policies are those of the countries with more than 30%

employment in agriculture, that is, a low level of economic development (industrialization)" (Wädekin, 1988: 324). Retrospectively, in Romania's case, Wädekin's prediction worked well.

The most important agrarian reform strategy adopted by the CAEM countries at the end of the 1960s and during the 1970s was referred to as the "industrialization of the agriculture". It consisted practically in the creation of large "agro-industrial complexes" (AIC) on the model of the western agribusiness. This was one of the new attempts to mimic market behavior by organizational means inside the planned, centralized economies of the communist bloc. The basic idea was to create backward and forward linkages to the rural cooperatives. The process was known as "vertical integration" and was supposed to better integrate the two sectors of the economy and to solve the multiple disequilibria problems between them.

The debates about the functions of the agro-industrial complexes were numerous and heated. They revealed the hopes that had been put by the communist leaders in organizational and socio-economic engineering. In the case of AIC, it was hopped that these will be able to fulfill the economic goal of increasing agricultural product and that their creation will limit the outflow of technically skilled labor from agriculture, as a result of the artificially created wage gap between the rural and urban sectors.

In Romania the creation of agro-industrial complexes debuted only in late 1976 while in the other East and Central European countries agro-industrial complexes had been already created on a mass scale roughly between 1968 and 1970. In Romania's case, the process was also more mimetic than elsewhere. The share of labor in the non-agricultural branches of the AIC remained lower in Romania than in the neighboring socialist countries. For instance, in the mid-1970s this share represented only 16% in Romania, 21% in Bulgaria but 30% in Hungary, 42% in Czechoslovakia and 53% in GDR (Wädekin, 1982: 237). Moreover, in Romania "decisive state influence through the administration of the state farms was maintained on all levels of such organizations" (Wädekin, 1982: 254). This situation was maintained until the late 1970s, when the state's intervention in the administration of the cooperatives was being revised and favored the strengthening of the forward linkages of agro-industrial complexes. The most important aspect of the administrative reorganization was the division of the Ministry of Agriculture and Food Industry into two distinct departments in 1979. The Industrial Processing of Agricultural Products department was responsible for the creation of forward linkages between the agro-industrial complexes and the food processing industries. However, much less attention was paid to the creation of backward linkages to the AIC, a situation that finally undermined the edifice of vertical integration.

During the 1980s, the weak performance of the State and cooperative-based agricultural sector across the CAEM countries could no longer be ignored. Contrary to the Marxist orthodoxy, the contribution of the very limited private agricultural sector to the total agricultural output was surprisingly high. For instance, in the mid-1980s the contribution of the private sector in Bulgaria was "about 25% of total agricultural output and about 34% of livestock output" (Cochrane, 1988: 243). It was shown that, overall, the private sector "has been almost completely responsible for the overall output growth during the 1980s" (Wyzan, 1988: 299). In Hungary the contribution of the private sector to the total agricultural output was even higher and represented about 34% in 1985 (Cochrane, 1988: 243). For the former Soviet Union studies of the contribution of the individual plots to the total production also indicated a very important contribution for the private sector (Severin, 1988; Hedlund, 1988). The private plots were estimated to "provide about a quarter of total agricultural output, on less than 3% of total sown area" (Hedlund, 1988: 216). The situation was paradoxal as, with Poland's exception where an estimated of 72.1% (Korbonski, 1988: 269) to 80% (Wädekin, 1982) of the land had been in private hands, in the rest of the Central and East European countries land was mainly held by large State or cooperative organizations.

The importance of the private rural sector began to be recognized in the Soviet Union also, first, in the Soviet Food Program of 1982 and more markedly after the March 1986 decree. A year later, in September 1987, the Central Committee of the Soviet Union issued a new decree "for improved conditions for private plot-holders" (Cochrane, 1988: 239). In general, this time the Soviet Union *followed* the reforms toward economic liberalization that were already pushed ahead by some East and Central European countries. It has been argued that Gorbachev's land measures had been inspired by the so-called New Economic Mechanism (NEM) that started to be revived in the 1980s in both Hungary and Bulgaria (Cochrane, 1988). The principles of the NEM referred to: greater enterprise autonomy, drastic reduction of the number of planning indicators in the management of economic units, the use of financial instruments to induce conformity to the national plans goals and greater autonomy in foreign trade decision-making at enterprise level. In various forms, these principles were adopted during the 1980s by all the CAEM countries.

As concerning Romania, in spite of the large contribution to the agricultural output of the otherwise limited private rural sector—in fact, the contribution of the private rural sector to the food supply was believed to have acted as a major political stabilizer during the food crisis period brought about by the forced export policy in the 1980s—the agrarian policy took a very different path from that in the neighboring Central and European countries. As Swinnen (1997) very well described the situation: "in the late 1970s and 1980s agriculture's special features under Ceausescu included severe limits on direct marketing of garden production by peasant and extensive exports of food and agricultural products. Consumption standards suffered more in Romania than in other countries. Ceausescu also forced upon the countryside a campaign to destroy the traditional villages and force peasant into high-rise concrete flats, often without amenities, in a 'village systematization program'. The aim of this program was to eliminate the peasant' independence spirit along with traditional elements of Romanian society" (Swinnen, 1997: 285). If the NEM principles were adopted in at least a mimetic way in industrial sectors, agriculture remained stalled in an old-fashioned centralism. In comparative terms, across the region, only in Albania was the situation probably worse, given the fact that the importance of the private rural sector had been completely denied in spite of the very severe food shortage that the country had begun to experience after 1985. Only about 0.5% of the arable land was privately owned, Albania being the only communist country in the region to have completely nationalized the land in the form of state property in 1976 (Cungu & Swinnen, 1999).

At a moment when the recognition and the spirit toward a certain liberalization of the economy was the common feature of the policy agenda in the Eastern European bloc, Romania, with its very peculiar state and communist party structure, completely centered around the president, followed a very different path of development that singularized it in the area.

6.3 Brief Outlook of the Romanian Agriculture at the End of the Communist Period

In 1989, the rural population in Romania represented 46.8% of the country's total population while 27.5% of the active labor force was employed in agriculture. From the perspective of a developed economy, the percentage was exceedingly high, but even compared to other CEE countries the percentage was still among the highest in Europe (Table 6.1).

As we have seen in Chap. 3, the high percentage of population employed in agriculture gave the Romanian land reform a peculiar character: combined with the fact that the restoration of private land ownership was based on the restitution principle (i.e. the restoration process followed the ownership structure that existed in agriculture by the start of collectivization in 1948) the foreseeable result of the land reform was the extreme fragmentation of land in plots with an average size of about 2.5 hectares. Over the next ten years, after the fall of communism, the fact was aggravated by a massive shift of over 10% of the active labor force from industry and tertiary sectors to agriculture as a result of the restructuration that took place in parallel in those sectors. Consequently, the ratio of agricultural land to population in Romania worked as one of the most restrictive factors for a successful land reform.

Table 6.1 Share of agriculture in total employment, 1989—selected countries

Country	(%)
Bulgaria	18.1
Czechoslovakia	9.9
German Democratic Republic	10.3
Hungary	11.0
Poland	25.8
Romania	27.5
Yugoslavia	17.0

Sources Swinnen (1994, p. 32, p. 216); Braverman et al. (1993, p. 208, p. 231, p. 247); Romanian Statistical Yearbook (1991)
Note Data for Yugoslavia are for 1988

Given the fact that the land reform took as a reference basis the already extremely fragmented land ownership structure that existed in the country in 1948 and that, in spite of the marked changes in the socio-demographic structure during the socialist era the proportion of the rural population remained high in Romania, the land reform was from its very beginning restricted by these structural parameters.

The communist regime brought, as one may expect, significant consequences for the structure of land ownership and the organization of production in agriculture. The ownership structure that characterized the Romanian agriculture during the socialist period changed little, once the difficult collectivization process ended in 1959. Private farming persisted in the mountainous areas and small plots of land were also privately farmed in the plains. In the 1980s, the area privately farmed was about 12.8% of the country's arable land (Brooks & Meurs, 1994). Theoretically, land has never been nationalized in Romania, but only contributed into collective farms. Although agricultural land was not formally nationalized, in practice peasants were not able to retain control over the plots they had been *forced* to bring into collective farms. None of the formal rights following from private ownership were respected and one could not pull out of collective farms. Consequently, for all practical matters, the legal status of land belonging to collective farms (CAPs) was not different from that belonging to state farms (IASs).

The restricted private farming sector aside, agricultural production was organized in two distinct forms: state and collective farms. By 1989, 2055 thousand hectares belonged to state farms that employed about 261 thousand persons. Other 8963 thousand hectares were farmed in collective farms by about 2 million peasants (Brooks & Meurs, 1994: 22). As mentioned, the main difference between the two was not in the form of land ownership but in the different degree to which they were endowed with machines and agricultural technology. In general, state farms benefited from a better endowment with agricultural machines, while collective farms relied more on labor-intensive techniques. Compared to other CEE countries, Romania had one of the lowest levels of agricultural mechanization—the share of active labor force employed in agriculture was high and the agricultural labor productivity measured as output per labor was low (Table 6.2).

Looking at the share of agriculture in the GDP in 1989 and in the total trade: in 1989 agriculture contributed 13.8% to Romania's GDP. Like Hungary and Bulgaria, Romania was a net exporter of agricultural products. However, the share of agricultural products in the total trade was lower in Romania than in the other CEE countries. In 1989 agriculture's share in the total trade was of only 4.1%. Agricultural exports represented 4.8% of the country's total exports and agricultural imports made up only 3.2% of Romania's total imports. Despite severe food shortages, the balance of agricultural trade was positive during the entire decade of the 1980s, and the agricultural imports represented an insignificant share of the country's imports.

To sum up, this chapter outlined the radical changes that took place in the realm of agrarian policy in Romania during the Communist period, as compared to the pre-1948 private property-based agriculture. It also highlighted the intellectual origins in the design of agrarian policies during this period as well as the constraints imposed by the totalitarian political system on the diffusion of alternative ideas about

Table 6.2 Agricultural labor productivity—selected countries

Country	Agricultural labor productivity (gross agricultural output/labor force), 1989 (in USD)	Relative labor productivity 1981–1985
Albania	431	–
Bulgaria	3749	58
Czech Republic	8063	–
Czechoslovakia	–	44
GDR	–	61
Hungary	6551	77
Poland	2389	51
Romania	2239	47
Slovakia	5743	–

Source Cungu and Swinnen (1999, p. 606); Braverman et al. (1993, p. 17)
Note The relative labor productivity is the net labor productivity in agriculture and forestry as a percentage of the net labor productivity in the nonagricultural sectors

agricultural development. We are now finally in the position to return to the recent past and to analyze in the next concluding chapter the extent to which the ideas and policy consequences of these two long periods of policy-making experiences were incorporated and influenced the post-1989 reforms in agriculture.

References

Braverman, A., Brooks, K. M., & Csaba, C. (Eds.). (1993). *The agricultural transition in Central and Eastern Europe and the Former USSR*. Washington, D.C., WA: World Bank.

Brooks, K., & Meurs, M. (1994). Romanian land reform: 1991–1993. *Comparative Economic Studies, 36*(2), 17–32.

Cochrane, N. J. (1988). Reforming socialist agriculture: Bulgarian and Hungarian experience and implications for the USSR. In K.-E. Wädekin (Ed.), *Communist agriculture: Farming in the Soviet Union and Eastern Europe* (pp. 233–250). New York, NY: Routledge.

Comisia Nationala de Statistica (CNS). (1991). *Romanian statistical yearbook*. Bucuresti: CNS.

Cungu, A., & Swinnen, J. F. M. (1999). Albania's radical agrarian reform. *Economic Development and Cultural Change, 47,* 605–620.

Hedlund, S. (1988). Private plots as a system stabilizer. In K.-E. Wädekin (Ed.), *Communist agriculture: Farming in the Soviet Union and Eastern Europe* (pp. 215–232). New York, NY: Routledge.

Johnson, G. D. (1993). Historical experience of East and Central European and Soviet agriculture. In A. Braverman, K. M. Brooks, & C. Csaba (Eds.), *The agricultural transition in Central and Eastern Europe and the Former USSR* (pp. 11–26). Washington, D.C., WA: World Bank.

Korbonski, A. (1988). Soldiers and peasants: Polish agriculture after martial rule. In K.-E. Wädekin (Ed.), *Communist agriculture: Farming in the Soviet Union and Eastern Europe* (pp. 279–289). New York, NY: Routledge.

Mitrany, D. (1951). *Marx against the peasant. A study in social dogmatism*. Chapel Hill, NC: University of North Carolina Press.

Murgescu, C. (1990). *Mersul Ideilor Economice la Români*. Bucuresti: Editura Enciclopedica.

Pryor, F. L. (1992). *The red and the green. The rise and fall of collectivized agriculture in marxist regimes*. Princeton, NJ: Princeton University Press.

Schultz, T. (1964). *Traditional agriculture*. New Haven, CT: Yale University Press.

Schultz, T. (1993). *The economics of being poor*. Cambridge, MA: Blackwell.

Severin, B. (1988). The March 1986 agricultural decree in perspective. In K.-E. Wädekin (Ed.), *Communist agriculture: Farming in the Soviet Union and Eastern Europe* (pp. 121–131). New York, NY: Routledge.

Swinnen, J. M. (Ed.). (1994). *Policy and institutional reform in Central European Agriculture*. Brookfield, VT: Avebury.

Swinnen, J. F. M. (1997). *Political economy of agrarian reform in Central and Eastern Europe*. Brookfield, VT: Ashgate.

Wädekin, K.-E. (1982). Agrarian policies in communist Europe. In E. M. Jacobs (Ed.), *A critical introduction* (Vol. I). Totowa, NJ: Allanheld, Osmun & Co.

Wädekin, K-E. (1988). Determinants and trends of reform in communist agriculture: A concluding essay. In K.-E. Wädekin (Ed.), *Communist agriculture: Farming in the Soviet Union and Eastern Europe* (pp. 321–331). New York, NY: Routledge.

Wyzan, M. L. (1988). Bulgarian agriculture: Sweeping reform, mediocre performance. In K.-E. Wädekin (Ed.), *Communist agriculture: Farming in the Soviet Union and Eastern Europe* (pp. 290–306). New York, NY: Routledge.

Chapter 7
Conclusions: Ideas and Policies in Comparative Historical Perspective

Abstract This chapter (Conclusions) sums up and synthetizes the insights from the previous chapters, focusing on the connection between on the one hand the ideas and policies about development that grew out in Romania and more generally in the space of Eastern Europe and, on the other hand the ideas, concepts and theories and policies originating in Western development economics. Then it moves to assess the Romanian development in relationship to the idea of policy learning. The focus is on evaluating the extent to which the ideas and policy consequences of the two long periods of policy-making experiences—the pre-communist and communist periods—were incorporated and influenced the post-1989 reforms in agriculture. The chapter concludes by pointing out future research directions that may further illuminate some core issues in understanding the Romanian experience and the phenomenon of agrarian reform in systems defined by economic and social dualism.

Keywords Marxism · Theory of economic development · Economic growth · Modernization · Western development economics · Soviet economics · New Economic Mechanism (NEM)

The previous chapters have demonstrated that many of the fundamental questions relevant to "late development" and structural economic change aimed at the modernization of societies defined by economic dualism, were already asked by the end of the 19th and the beginning of the twentieth century. We have seen that some of the long-lasting questions of the development literature were being asked at the start of the modernization process and have periodically reemerged up to the present: What should be the relationship between the two major sectors of a dual economy—agriculture and industry? What is the role of farm size in economic productivity? What is the adequate form of production organization in agriculture? How can agriculture contribute to the development of industry? Could development (and especially late development) be conceptualized as a "center-periphery" relationship between "advanced" and "backward" countries?

All these questions become recurrent themes in development economics and rural sociology and persisted, if not dominated, the debates about development for the rest of the century. Also, the main policy solutions to those questions were articulated and

A. Dabu and P. D. Aligica, *Economic Dualism and Agrarian Policies*, SpringerBriefs in Economics, https://doi.org/10.1007/978-3-030-47836-0_7

were the object of practical experiments during both the pre-communist and post-communist periods. As such, in conjunction, they offered a huge learning potential regarding development strategy and agricultural reform in the post 1989 decade. Yet, as this study demonstrated, the post-communist policymakers used that potential only to a limited extent. In doing that, the study ended up revisiting a significant segment of the Romanian agrarian history. At the same time, it has opened the way to an exploration in concrete ways of the position that ideas and rational learning—understood as policymaking informed by previous policy experiences—had in this particular area of post-communist policy making.

To get a better sense of the broader significance and relevance and insights offered, the concluding section of the book will focus on the connection between on the one hand, the ideas and policies about development that grew out in Romania (and more generally in the space of Eastern Europe and the Soviet Union) and, on the other hand, the ideas, concepts, theories and policies originating in Western development economics, a field that established itself as a distinct branch of economics in the 1950s. In this respect, two observations are relevant regarding the lessons of over half a century of systematic research by developmental economists and sociologists.

First, in Eastern Europe and Romania in particular, efforts to theorize the process of development in agrarian countries long preceded the emergence of development economics (Love 1996). Incipient ideas about the process of development had already been formulated as early as the second half of the nineteenth century and had been more fully developed into theories and policy solutions in the first half of the twentieth century.

Second, it is noteworthy that the emergence of development economics as a distinct field at the end of World War II, was concomitant with the shift to planned economies and planned agriculture in the countries of Eastern Europe. This situation resulted in a much more limited impact of development economics in Eastern Europe, given the fact that most of the development models and policies followed from neo-classical assumptions and assumed an economic system based on private property. Although this could constitute a research project in itself, we could claim—based on the current knowledge—that, to a certain extent, there was overlap in the ideas about development as well as a coincidence in the reasons that generated policy shifts in both the planned and market economies in the second half of the twentieth century. Divergence between the two economic systems registered mainly at the level of policy solutions and implementation. One could support this claim by simply comparing the moments in agricultural policy shifts in the CMEA (Comecon) countries (and by extension in Romania) in the post war period with the changes in development paradigms and policy shifts in the field of development economics per se. The comparative analysis will put in a broader and deeper perspective the insights gained so far through our investigation of the Romanian case study.

Several authors (Timmer, 1998; Mellor, 1998; Staatz & Eicher, 1998) remarked that the emergence to salience in the 1950s of a number of development theories emphasizing the role of industry in economic growth, led to the view that agriculture was the lagging sector of the economy, unable to generate growth or efficiency gains. The major consequence of this view was the rise of the so-called "squeeze agriculture" paradigm (Timmer, 1998) as the prevailing theoretical framework for policy design in many developing countries in the 1950s. Structural change of the economy became equated with underinvestment in agriculture and emphasis on the need for the growth of the industrial sector with almost no regard for any of the long-run social, economic or political consequences of this policy. Staatz and Eicher (1990) sum up the situation as follows:

> Most Western development economists of the 1950s did not view agriculture as an important contributor to economic growth. […] The role of development economics was seen as facilitating that transformation [of the structural transformation of the economy] by discovering ways to transfer resources, especially labor, from traditional agriculture to industry, the presumed engine of growth. Agriculture itself was often treated as a "black box" from which people, and food to feed them, and perhaps capital could be released (Staatz & Eicher, 1990, 4).

They also show how a range of theoretical arguments framed in the 1950s and built upon distinct theoretical assumptions, converged in their policy implications and conveyed an industrial orientation to many countries' development agenda. Chief elements in this policy shift were the publication of the dual economy model by Lewis in 1954, the conceptualization by Hirschman of the "linkage effect" (and his assertion that agriculture has weak capability to generate linkage effects, and spawn subsequent investments in other sectors of the economy), and the Prebisch and Singer thesis of unfavorable terms of trade for agricultural products (with the policy implication that the accent should fall on the development of national industries).

Whether or not these ideas were influential in the designs of development programs in the CMEA countries in the 1950s or they just happened to coincide in terms of policy recommendations with the Marxist tenet of the superiority of industry and innate inefficiency of the private farming sector (or in the case of Romania, with the theory of unequal exchange formulated in the 1930s by Manoilescu—a precursor of the dependency perspectives of ECLA-European Commission for Latin American) is a separated topic. What is worth nothing however is the coincidental "push on industry" (Mellor, 1998) that followed from both the Western development economics and the Marxist doctrine in the 1950s. As Timmer (1998) put it: "The unique features of agriculture as a sector were simply not widely understood in the 1950s. Nor was it accepted that the development of modern agriculture was necessary as a concomitant to development of the rest of the economy" (123). Obviously, the policies to "squeeze" agriculture differed markedly in market versus planned economies. In the former, taxation and indirect intervention in the price structure of agricultural products was favored. In the latter, coercion was more direct: socialization of the private property, forced quotas and requisitions, and centrally fixed prices did the job.

In the 1960s and more markedly during the 1970s, the need for increased agricultural output to sustain industrial development came to be recognized in both the West and the CMEA countries. The idea that the change of a country's economic structure and the growth of its industrial sector were not independent from improvements in agriculture's capacity to increase output and to meet an ever-rising demand for food, translated into a new paradigm and policy shift. The paradigm shift had been announced by the new emphasis "on '*role*' rather than the mere '*contribution*' of agriculture" (Timmer, 1998: 123). In policy terms, the need to invest in agriculture began to be recognized. This is what Timmer called, after the names of the most influential scholars who introduced this pivotal conceptual shift, "the Johnston-Mellor environment" for the role of agriculture in development.

In an article written in 1961, Johnston and Mellor identified five possible roles that agriculture could play in economic growth and that could set a country's process of development on a path of firm and unremitting progress: (1) increase the supply of food, (2) provide labor to the industrial sector, (3) raise the demand for industrial output, (4) increase the supply of savings in the economy, (5) finance capital acquisition for industry through agricultural exports (Timmer, 1998: 123). Many of the roles for agriculture identified by Johnston and Mellor indicate a certain continuity with the prior "extractive" orientation towards agriculture. Nevertheless, what was new in economics was the transition from a priori theorizing towards empirical research (Staatz & Eicher, 1998). Their position generated thus a policy shift that what favoring investment in agriculture and "balanced growth" or, in other words, a better integration of agriculture and industry through both labor and product markets. The need to better integrate the two sectors, it was shown, becomes more stringent as the share of a country's labor force employed in agriculture declines, and the extraction of labor from agriculture becomes more problematic.

Once that point is reached, a new shift in policy occurs, one that demands the "integration of agriculture into the macro-economy" (or, as Timmer put it, "the Schultz-Ruttan environment"). At this stage, agriculture is linked to the overall economy through the better development of labor and credit markets that can assuage the shock of the increasing income gap between agriculture and industry. However, a negative side effect of this policy was the increased vulnerability of the agricultural sector to the macro-economic fluctuations in prices, and aggregate demand and supply.

Wädekin (1982) described a similar change of perspective regarding the role of agriculture in development for the CMEA countries. However, this similarity need not be stretched beyond a number of common elements and ideas that can be easily identified. Wädekin described the mechanisms by which underinvestment in agriculture came to be recognized as a counter-productive policy, one that if continued, could in the end jeopardize the growth of the industrial sector itself. Several elements contributed to this understanding. First, the peculiarities of planning in agriculture came to be recognized. As Wädekin noted: "In agriculture more than in any other branch of the economy, the rigid and centralized planning was unable to take into account the diversity of climate, soil, and social and economic conditions at the local and regional level" (1982: 205). In this respect, development economics had undergone a similar turn of perspective. For instance, it was recognized that: "the early purposeful neglect of agriculture can in part be attributed to development economists who were remote from any real understanding of what makes the agriculture sector quite different from either manufacturing or services" (Timmer, 1998: 125). That being said, once the distinctive character of agriculture, as compared to other sectors of the economy, was acknowledged, development economics went into a much more productive research direction than what the economics of planned agriculture could possibly undergo. For instance, the microeconomic approach focusing on the analysis of farm household behavior, the study of decision-making in agriculture, and the analysis of land tenure systems for agricultural output, became more predominant in the study of the rural economy.

When, across the CMEA countries, the peculiarities of planning in agriculture could no longer be ignored, the focus of policy makers shifted on diminishing, the number of plan indicators and granting the state- and the collective-cooperative farms more autonomy and flexibility in their operation. Interestingly, the former Stalinist, ultra-centralized operation of the farms "worked more or less, so long as soil and unskilled labor continued to be available in abundance" (Wädekin, 1982: 206). Apparently, the intuition behind Lewis' model of a dual economy was confirmed under conditions of central planning, in the sense that the Stalinist system could no longer operate beyond the so-called "shortage point" of a dual economy—that is to say, the point beyond which the continuation of labor outflow from agriculture would be associated with decline in the agricultural output. It came to be clearly appreciated that unless labor productivity in agriculture would increase, the terms of trade for agricultural products would be set against industry.

Two distinct phenomena seemed to have triggered the pressure for an upward move in the prices of agricultural products. First, an increase in the monetary incomes of the urban sector that was not met by an adequate supply of non-food products (and, in particular, consumer goods). Second, a decline of output in agriculture as a result of lagging labor productivity. This was the main mechanism by which greater investment in agriculture and a more flexible organization of the state and collective farms came to be regarded as desirable policy shifts. At the same time, as Wädekin (1982) insightfully notices, these were the reasons that induced a shift of paradigm similar to the one produced in the Western development economics: away from the view of agriculture as a contributor to growth, toward agriculture as a full player in the process of growth. As he put it: "The diverging developments of incomes and food supply, combined with rapid urbanization and the insufficient diversion of income increments to nonfood commodities, demonstrate that *the situation was and is not merely a problem of food production. It is even more one of the economy at large, and of the role attributed to agriculture*" (Wädekin, 1982, 104, emphasis added).

In a free market economy, the less-than-unitary income elasticity for the demand of agricultural products lessens the pressure for upward move of the agricultural prices. In a planned economy, the pervasive shortage of various nonfood products makes the levy of the income elasticity less relevant as the consumer choices are strictly limited by what is actually available on the shelf, and at any given moment, not much is (Timmer, 1998: 115; Wädekin, 1982: 102–3). The bottom line is that in both market and planned economies, the role of agriculture in the process of development started to become more central despite the very different sets of arguments that gave rise later on to a policy shift, arguing for the need to better integrate agriculture with industry, also known as the "industrialization of agriculture paradigm".

This brief comparative overview of the approaches to the role of agriculture in development, as articulated in the CMEA countries and in the field of development economics, had the sole intention to show that *some ideas and policy recommendations may be powerful enough to reproduce themselves even under such radically different systems of economic organization as the plan and the market.* Obviously, the intention of the above discussion was not to equate the achievements of the two "fields". It goes without saying that the conceptualization and theorization of development in the CMEA countries was much more restricted by ideological tenets and political obstacles that inhibited the open inquiry into the process of economic development, in a way unknown to Western scholars of development economics. The contrived limitation of ideas and the subsequent scarcity of effective policy solutions to the issue of economic and social underdevelopment during the period of planned agriculture in Romania and elsewhere are notorious by now and our book highlighted this aspect.

We have reached now the point of summing up. The tables below offer a synthesis of the ideas, theories, policies, and lessons that characterized the pre-communist and communist periods in the Romanian experience of dealing with agricultural underdevelopment: (Tables 7.1 and 7.2).

Once equipped with the above synthesis, the answer to the question "to what extent could we speak of a policy learning process in the post 1989 agrarian reforms of Romania between 1990 and 2000", could be re-framed in a clearer and straightforward manner. Almost none of the major lessons emerging from the communist and pre-communist periods seem to have been incorporated into the post-communist policy design processes.

For instance, in spite of the fact that the lessons of both pre-1989 periods converged in the conclusion that land redistribution alone is a very imperfect solution to the improvement of economic efficiency in agriculture, post-1989 reformers made pure land redistribution the cornerstone of their reforms. Seen in the light of the present research, the downbeat results were quite unsurprising. In fact, the study reveals that a suppressed tension permanently existed between the declared policy-orientation—a private agriculture—and the actual policy options followed in practice. Although the restitution principle was followed, substantial State support continued to go to the *State*-owned agricultural sector (for instance 80 percent of the subsidized credits), and the process of privatizing the large state agricultural enterprises (IASs) was slow and permanently delayed.

In a similar way, the pre-communist-period experience teaches that although the private cooperation system could be the solution to land fragmentation and large rural population, the high instability of the legislation of rural cooperation discouraged the attempts toward organization into cooperatives. The same kind of legislative uncertainty reigned after 1989, during the decade that is the object of our study. In this case, there was no excuse as no significant roadblock was manifest against the legislation in question. It was a mere failure of policy insight and even of common sense. Moreover, the legislation directly favored the *continuation* of the former cooperative organizations and was unsupportive of the creation of new cooperatives that would be based on free association of members on their own choice. The law did not ban the creation of such cooperatives, but it did not offer incentives for the establishment

Table 7.1 Ideas, theories, policies, and lessons—the pre-communist period (1864–1948)

Ideas/Theories	Policies/Policy recommendations	Results	Lessons/Implications
Landownership is a political right	Land reform and redistribution	Dismantling of the large latifundia End of feudal relationships in agriculture	Land redistribution alone is a very imperfect solution to the improvement of economic efficiency in agriculture
Increases in agricultural production can be realized by expanding the area under cultivation and via improvements in the cropping systems such as crop-rotation, use of organic manures		Political and social status of the peasants gradually improves: rights to vote and to political participation are granted	The "frontier" and "conservation" models of agriculture reach their limits once the output growth rate is superseded by the rate of population growth
		Agricultural output increases but the economic welfare of the peasants is stagnant or worsens	
Large farms are more productive than small farms and can better capture economies of scale	Collectivization and dismantling of the peasant holdings-based agriculture	General aversion by the peasant class to socialist ideas	The Marxist-Populist debate ensued No clear lessons
The law of capital concentration will inexorably destroy the peasant rural society			
Peasant farms represent a distinct, resilient, and economically superior form of work and production organization in agriculture	Emphasis on industry's development is not suitable, Romania lacks the necessary historical conditions that would lead her to follow in the steps of advanced industrial nations	Rural credit continued to be very limited; the majority of peasants lacked the means to guarantee their credit	Strong State intervention in the cooperative movement, political manipulation, and bureaucratization of its entire territorial structure pervert the objectives of voluntary cooperation

(continued)

Table 7.1 (continued)

Ideas/Theories	Policies/Policy recommendations	Results	Lessons/Implications
The Marxist law of capital concentration does not apply to agriculture. The fundaments of the political organization of Romania should be a "peasant state"	The development of rural cooperation and, in particular, of credit cooperatives Private property rights to land are to be maintained	Only a few production cooperatives establish on a voluntary basis	High instability of the legislation of rural cooperation discourages the attempts for organization into cooperatives
Peasants constitute a sociologically distinct part of the society, culturally distinct from the small segment of the population employed in industry	There is not much to be done in policy terms	Skepticism about Romania's practical possibility to catch up with the developed world	A form of Boekean "sociological dualism" pervades the writings on economic backwardness in Romania. Dualist models lead to policy inaction

of new cooperatives either, as it did not allow for the transfer of the capital of former cooperatives toward the newly formed ones.

Finally, during the 1990s the disjuncture between the agricultural and industrial sector deepened, despite efforts made during the previous decades for their closer integration. Neither the supplying industries, nor the beneficiary industries were sufficiently well connected to the agricultural sector and in fact the new large private agricultural sector remained almost isolated, a situation that aggravated the subsistence orientation of the Romanian agriculture.

To sum up, the degree to which the post 1989 agrarian reforms were influenced by the policy experiences and ideas of the previous periods was extremely limited, almost negligible. To the extent that one may speak of a policy learning process in the post 1989 agrarian reforms, it is a learning process devoid of a systematic exposure to and understanding of the theoretical fundamentals of the polices taken as a learning source. That is to say, the study disconfirms the conjecture that the ideas, concepts, and theories that led to policy failure and mixed results in the past were rejected or correspondingly adjusted to the new context. At most, the rational policy-making model, based on the strong notion of conceptual learning, seems to be able to offer just a benchmark. This benchmark could help us to start addressing alternative hypotheses about the phenomena of interest but cannot take us very far beyond that.

For instance, although the present analysis has not directly discussed the role played by various interest groups, their pervasive influence in the process of agricultural law making has been pointed out repeatedly. That suggests a political science

Table 7.2 Ideas, theories, policies, and lessons—the communist period (1948–1989)

Ideas/Theories	Policies/Policy recommendations	Results	Lessons/Implications
Large collective farms represent the best way of organizing production in agriculture	Forced collectivization of agriculture	Land and agricultural machinery become State property	In the absence of clear property rights to land and agricultural output, the large farm size does not operate economically
The abolition of the institution of private property of land and of means of production leads to increases of output and labor productivity		During the first two decades of planned agriculture output and productivity growth was obtained, but the trend could not be sustained	Evidence about the productivity of the small plots during the period of planned agriculture supports the above conclusion. Also, at a micro-level, it shows that peasants do behave 'rationally' and react to economic incentives
Agriculture—a source of financing industrial development	Agriculture 'squeezing' policies: Under-investment in agriculture machinery coupled with the maintenance of a relatively large labor force in agriculture	Extensive growth of agricultural output	Capital investment in agriculture is necessary to support industrial development; one cannot take place in the absence of the other
	Maintenance of artificially low prices for agricultural products coupled with a large agriculture-industry wage gap	Once the sources for an extensive growth were exhausted, stagnation/decline in agricultural output followed	
Industrialization of agriculture	Vertical integration of agriculture and industry: creation of agro-industrial complexes	Mixed results: Increased attention for agriculture's capitalization needs	The idea that it is necessary to create "input-output" links between the two sectors is a very useful one. This integration process however can be damaged if seen as a "distributive", non-market process
		Improvement of the distribution channels for agricultural products, but insufficient connection with input industries	

and public choice perspective. Initially, the main pivot of political action has been represented by the villages' former "nomenklatura", and this has put its stamp on the process of agricultural law making in the post-1989 period. Accordingly, it would be interesting to identify and assess the social composition, social organization, political strength, and organizational structure of the new interest groups that were formed during the first decade of post-communism. Equally important would be to identify and to explore the latent and manifest sociological functions of the formal channels through which such groups eventually influenced agricultural policy making in Romania.

Equally interesting would be to take a closer look and challenge the "legalistic" approach—i.e. the naïve expectation that if a body of legislation would be adopted, a series of actions and desirable consequences would automatically follow. For over a century, this formulaic approach was a constant feature of all the policies intended for economic and in particular, agricultural development in Romania. As has been amply shown in this book, this "legalistic" formulaic attitude toward the process of agricultural development, and the consequent expectations it raised, have been repeatedly frustrated by the reality of the unfolding agricultural developments on the ground. Applying the tools of institutional analysis in order to look at the actual structure of property rights, the prevalent tenancy arrangements, and the main forms of agricultural production organization that were in fact gaining ground in Romania, as well as to the political economy of their operational environment, may be a possible way out of the mechanics of the "legalistic" mindset. As the present study has pointed out, many institutional arrangements that dominated the organization of production in the countryside were not well understood, were not mapped out, and were often ignored due to their "informal" character. An analysis inspired by institutional theory, could underscore the importance of these arrangements and of their relationship to their political economy environment, and, by doing that, it could help to overcome the formulaic approach so deeply rooted in the Romanian tradition of agricultural policy-making. But these and other related approaches are a topic of an entirely separated discussion and investigation.

References

Mellor, J. W. (1998). Agriculture on the road to industrialization. In C. K. Eicher & J. M. Staatz (Eds.), *International agricultural development* (pp. 136–54). Baltimore: The John Hopkins University Press.

Love, J. L. (1996). *Crafting the third world development: Theorizing underdevelopment in Rumania and Brazil*. Stanford, CA: Stanford University Press.

Staatz, J. M., & C. K. Eicher. (1990). Agricultural development ideas in historical perspective. In C. K. Eicher & J. M. Staatz (Eds.), *International agricultural development* (pp. 3–40). Baltimore, ML: The John Hopkins University Press.

Staatz, J. M., & C. K. Eicher. (1998). Agricultural development ideas in historical perspective. In C. K. Eicher & J. M. Staatz (Eds.), *International agricultural development* (pp. 8–38). Baltimore,ML: The John Hopkins University Press.

Timmer, P. (1998). The agricultural transformation. In C. K. Eicher & J. M. Staatz (Eds.), *International agricultural development* (pp. 113–135). Baltimore, ML: The John Hopkins University Press.

Wädekin, K.-E. (1982). Agrarian policies in communist Europe. In E. M. Jacobs (Ed.), *A critical introduction* (Vol. I). Totowa, NJ: Allanheld, Osmun & Co.

The manufacturer's authorised representative in the EU is Springer Nature Customer Service Centre GmbH, Europaplatz 3, 69115 Heidelberg, Germany. If you have any concerns regarding our products, please contact ProductSafety@springernature.com

Printed and bound by CPI Group (UK) Ltd, Croydon, CR0 4YY

30/09/2026

02225606-0010